# PEDALING THROUGH
# PROVENCE
## COOKBOOK

## SARAH LEAH CHASE
### ILLUSTRATED BY
### LINDA MONTGOMERY

WORKMAN PUBLISHING, NEW YORK

Nice

Gordes

Les Baux

Grignan

Ménerbes

Thanks to the following for permission to use the excerpts selected for this book: **Page IX:** *The Rough Guide to Provence & The Côte d'Azur* by Kate Baillie. Copyright © 1992 by Kate Baillie. Reprinted by permission of Rough Guides Ltd. **Page 2:** *Cuisine of the South of France* by Roger Vergé. Copyright © 1980 by Roger Vergé. Reprinted by permission of William Morrow and Company, Inc. **Page 41:** *The Wonderful Food of Provence* by Jean Noel Escudier and Peta J. Fuller. Copyright © 1968 by Robert Rebstock and Peta J. Fuller. Reprinted by permission of Houghton Mifflin Co. All rights reserved. **Page 45:** *Food of France* by Waverley Root. Copyright © 1977 by Waverley Root. Reprinted by permission of Random House, Inc. **Page 113:** *Adventures on the Wine Route: A Wine Buyer's Tour of France* by Kermit Lynch. Copyright © 1988 by Kermit Lynch. Reprinted by permission of Farrar, Straus & Giroux, Inc. **Page 170:** *A Taste of Provence* by Carey & Julian More. Copyright © 1988 by Carey & Julian More. Reprinted by permission of Pavilion Books. **Page 174:** *Toujours Provence* by Peter Mayle. Copyright © 1991 by Peter Mayle. Reprinted by permission of Random House, Inc. **Page 178:** *Caesar's Vast Ghost— Aspects of Provence* by Lawrence Durrell. Copyright © 1990 by Lawrence Durrell. Reprinted by permission of Arcade Publishing.

**Library of Congress Cataloging-in-Publication Data**
Chase, Sarah Leah.
Pedaling through Provence cookbook / by Sarah Leah Chase;
illustrations by Linda Montgomery.
p. cm.
Includes index.
ISBN 0-7611-0233-7
1. Cookery, French—Provençal style. 2. Cookery—France—Provence. 3. Bicycle touring—France—Provence. 4. Provence (France)—Description and travel. I. Title.
TX719.2.P754C49 1995
641.59449—dc20
95-32831
CIP

Cover design by Lisa Hollander
Book design by Lisa Hollander with Lori S. Malkin
Cover and book illustrations by Linda Montgomery

Workman books are available at special discounts when purchased in bulk for premium and sales promotions as well as for fund-raising or educational use. Special editions or book excerpts can also be created to specification. For details, contact the Special Sales Director at the address below.

Workman Publishing Company, Inc.
708 Broadway, New York, NY 10003-9555

First printing October 1995
10 9 8 7 6 5 4 3 2 1

IN MEMORY OF CAREY BRIDGERS, who I know has found a paradise akin to the South of France.

# acknowledgments

researching this Provence cookbook has been like sipping a glass of Côtes de Provence rosé and having it too. If only all work were so pleasurable! I continue to extend heartfelt thanks to those at Workman Publishing and Butterfield & Robinson Travel who have aided and abetted my many pleasures in working on this cookbook in my *Pedaling* series. At Workman, acknowledgment is gleefully due my publisher Peter Workman and editor Suzanne Rafer, designer Lisa Hollander and her associate Lori Malkin, and publicist Andrea Glickson. This book and this series simply would not exist without the enthusiatic support of George Butterfield at Butterfield & Robinson. Additionally, my transatlantic travels and research are always made smoother thanks to the expert help and advice of B&R staffers Nicola Speakman, M. G. Eaton, Victoria Bake, and Nathalie Bichot. I am indebted to you all.

Linda Montgomery merits especially appreciative praise for the evocative liveliness her terrific illustrations have brought to my Provençal tales and recipes. I've loved previewing each and every sketched vignette, from the first sensuous bottle of rosé wine to the last little sprig of lavender!

One grand ratatouille's worth of gratitude gets ladled to the eclectic array of friends and new acquaintances who have enriched my Provençal experiences in myriad ways. Thanks to Lori and Helen, and Bill and Cheryl for putting a comfortable bed and heavenly Provençal kitchen at my eager disposal *chez* La Tuilerie in the Var. Carey Bridgers and Jonathan Green made the greatest of co-guides and companions throughout the bicycle trips we led together in Provence. I'm delighted to have recently established a warm culinary connection with Nito and David Carpita at their Mas de Cornud in St.-Rémy and am particularly grateful for their sharing of

recipes, insights, and nightcaps alike. Since I truly believe "life is nothing without garlic," I'm elated that most of my Nantucket dinner party guests along with the students who attend my summer cooking classes concur. Speaking of and reeking of garlic, aromatic thanks are extended to Anna Sortun for so readily sharing her fabulous *aïgo bouïdo* recipe. At home, over the past year or so, when I haven't been grinding my pestle against a mortar to churn out *aïolis, anchoïades,* or *pistous,* I've been chopping up a storm to make *salades niçoises, daubes,* and *tians,* and that is always made that much easier with a Fred DeCarlo sharpened knife in hand.

Finally, I offer admiring thanks to all the talented writers, poets, painters, chefs, and wine *aficionados* whose personal homages to beloved Provence have enriched, enlightened, and expanded my own ever-increasing affection for that happy, sun-and-sea-saturated province in the South of France.

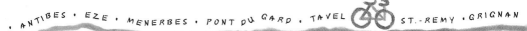

# contents

༄

## ſenſationaL ſpreadſ, ſauceſ, and ſipſ of the ſun . . . . . . . . . .1

THESE OLIVE-FLECKED, ANCHOVY-PACKED, anything-but-subtle starters exude the flavors of sun-drenched cuisine and invoke thirsts readily slaked by Provence's refreshing libations.

## ſoulful ſoupſ . . . .35

A *VIBRANT BOWL OF SOUP*—whether based on the sweet simplicity of a tomato or the rich variety of the Mediterranean—is a time-honored Provençal tradition and comfort.

## provençaL paſtaſ, pizzaſ, and ſundry ſavorieſ . . . . . . . . . . . . . .57

PROVENCE'S BRIGHT, BOLD BISTRO, beach, and street fare gives a culinary nod to neighboring Italy.

# falling in Love with provence

THE ANCIENT PROVENÇAL VERSION OF GENESIS maintains that prior to introducing Adam, the Creator realized he had several materials left over: large expanses of celestial blue, all kinds of rocks, arable soil filled with seeds for a sumptuous flora, and a variety of as yet unused tastes and smells from the most subtle to the most powerful. "Well," He thinks, "Why don't I make a beautiful resumé of my world, my own special paradise?" And so Provence came into being.

—KATE BAILLIE
*THE ROUGH GUIDE'S PROVENCE & THE CÔTE D'AZUR*

ix

I have become passionate about Provence. Many people are, including an inspiring array of accomplished artists, writers, poets, designers, and, of course, mentor cookbook authors.

My first trip to the South of France took me only to the Côte d'Azur and occurred just after I had graduated from college. I had flown to France to guide a Butterfield & Robinson student bicycling adventure that kicked off with a week's immersion in a French language course in Nice. Fresh from my studies, I was filled with anticipatory and romanticized visions of a Riviera frozen in time between the Belle Epoque, F. Scott Fitzgerald's "tender nights" in Cap d'Antibes, Cole Porter's pleasure-loving lyrics, and Ernest Hemingway's *Garden of Eden.* I expected to be enveloped by the light of the Impressionist painters and see the dazzling colors of Van Gogh's, Cézanne's,

Matisse's, and Picasso's famed canvases dancing everywhere. Once I arrived, it did not take long to become a little disillusioned and to begin to grasp that there is indeed as much myth as there is magic to this Mediterranean coastline.

My first rendezvous in Nice was with a former college friend who had spent the year there on a Rotary fellowship. His initial excitement had gradually turned to frustration with the rigidity of many of the set French ways and to despair over the staid retirement community aura, which he claimed now permeated Nice during the winter months. He had countered by seeking the company of any bohemians he could find. And that is how I came to spend my first afternoon in Nice in a very steamy and dark, unimpressionistic apartment, where various angst-driven artistic souls wandered about in a state of complete nakedness dropping occasional fragments of philosophical French thought. I tried in vain to put myself at ease; perhaps I was bearing witness to the sort of scene that might have inspired Picasso's painting of *Les Demoiselles d'Avignon*. My clothes, which I kept on, and my awkward textbook French made me blush and perspire unbearably. I at once yearned to be back in the security of my collegiate ivy tower, where the avant-garde was merely contemplated or discussed, not acted upon.

Fortunately, the dinner hour loomed, and with this impetus to search out a meal, came my first glimpse of a Côte d'Azur I would grow to love and return to again and again. Compared with the gloom of that apartment, any sort of daylight would have seemed especially welcoming, but the resplendent light that greeted me on this early evening in Nice was truly remarkable. My earlier longings for the familiar security of New Eng-

x
...

land's bricks and dull gray shingles were quickly erased and replaced with sheer glee at seeing the soft pink and peach of Nice's palm-, plane-, and pine-tree-fringed villas cascading down gentle green hills toward the azure Mediterranean. A walk along the city's famed and flowered waterfront Promenade des Anglais past the persimmon-colored dome and pistachio turrets of the grand Negresco Hotel whetted my appetite further for our dining destination in Vieux Nice, or Old Nice. There, among the canopied stalls of the open-air market on the Cours Saleya, the cafés and restaurants were numerous and enticingly animated. And the impending twilight air was intoxicating with its mingling scents of savory herbs, sweet flowers, lusty anchovies and olives, and briny fresh fish. My introduction to *pastis,* the region's potent anise-flavored *apéritif,* was met with an initial resistance, though I would later come not only to acquire a taste for it but also to adore it. The freshly caught fish I proceeded to order for dinner—simply but perfectly grilled with *herbes de Provence* and golden olive oil—planted those first divine seeds hinting at the sort of sybaritic pleasures that would soon come to highlight this and all my future sojourns to the South of France.

The students on my trip arrived a few days later and began their routine of intensive morning language studies. While they were in class, I spent my free time taking delightful daily pilgrimages to the seventeenth-century Villa des Arènes, which houses Nice's Matisse Museum. Matisse's joyful and vibrant paintings and cut-outs thrilled me and I soon found myself viewing every newly visited place along the Riviera through an imagined Matisse perspective. I loved walking along the old sea walls of Antibes and continuing out on the curvy road to the chic hotels, gardens, and beaches of its *cap.* Cannes, however, was too glitzy for me and Juan-les-Pins too cheesy. The rampant commercialism of the supposedly quaint St.-Paul-de-Vence shocked, while the seldom-mentioned village of Villeneuve-Loubet—known only because it was the birthplace of the famed chef Auguste Escoffier—charmed with its sweet Musée de l'Art Culinaire. Traveling the sinuous and breathtakingly beautiful *corniche* roads skirting the Alpes-Maritimes between Nice and Monaco made me feel as glamorous and daring as Grace Kelly in the movies of her Hollywood heyday. It's only a shame that I never could conclude which spectacular resort village would be perfect for my wish-list-in-another-life villa—the old fishing port of Villefranche or exclusive St.-Jean-Cap-Ferrat, boat-bountiful Beaulieu or exquisitely perched Eze.

After the students completed their weeklong language course in Nice, we departed, according to the trip's design, to bicycle in other parts of France.

It was not until 1986 that I came to experience the profound pleasures of biking on Provençal soil. At the time, I ran a restaurant on Nantucket Island, and come autumn, annually guided one of Butterfield & Robinson's newly designed adult biking tours. Provence was on the agenda for September, and Labor Day couldn't pass quickly enough to free me and my co-guide, a French-speaking waiter from my restaurant, for our rejuvenating three weeks of research and cycling.

Butterfield & Robinson's cycling routes understandably did not go anywhere near the crazed *corniches* of the Côte d'Azur, but instead concentrated on those inland areas that many have long considered the true Provence, in the rich and varied *départements* of the Vaucluse and the Bouches-du-Rhône. I traveled to this part of Provence with culinary expectations but without the preconceived notions of place I had previously projected on the Riviera. With its awesome and pervasive remnants of Roman civilization, I found a province far more ancient than I ever would have imagined. Yet, at the same time, everything that was so unchanged somehow managed to seem impeccably chic. The landscape of the countryside alternated between parched and perched, barren and bacchanalian. Likewise, the food had its range between magnificently Mediterranean and disappointingly mundane. The cycling, however, always infused with some scent or another to be swooned over—from piny rosemary and laven-der to sun-saturated tomatoes and melons to heady garlic and olives and yeasty sweet wine grapes—it was, in a word, sublime. From the first warm-up spin across the ancient and awesome Pont du Gard

to the huff-and-puff biking up to Les Baux to my *aïoli* picnics in the fertile fields between Cavaillon and Carpentras, it became easy to relate to the perfectly expressed Provençal sentiments of French writer Michel del Castillo: "You feel you would like to remain there forever but also that you've probably been there for centuries."

I have now bicycled many times through an ever-growing, impas-sioned list of places in inland Provence. I sympathize enthusiastical-ly with those who insist that plane-tree-shaded St.-Rémy is the best village in all of Provence. The wonderful walking tour, after all, to the still exquisitely intact iris gardens, olive groves, and stonewalled fields of Van Gogh's St.-Rémy paintings remains an all-time favorite tour of mine. At the same time, however, it is hard not to pledge an equally exclusive love to lively canal-crisscrossed L'Isle-sur-la-Sorgue, or, for that matter, any of the quintessentially perched villages of the laid-back Lubéron—Gordes, Roussillon, Lacoste, and Ménerbes. But then I'd be neglecting to mention how much I adore meandering on two wheels through the wine villages of Tavel, Châteauneuf-du-Pape, Gigondas, Vacqueyras, and Beaumes-de-Venise. And, there is noth-

France
Provence
Italy
Valence
Rhône
Grignan
Nyons
Vaison-la-Romaine
Gigondas
Orange
Vacqueyras
Crillon-le-Brave
Tavel
Châteauneuf-du-Pape
Beaumes-de-Venise
Sault
Uzès
Avignon
Carpentras
Gordes
Pont du Gard
L'Isle-sur-la-Sorgue
St.-Rémy
Lacoste
Ménerbes
Les Baux
Moustiers-Ste.-Marie
Fontvieille
Maussane-les-Alpilles
Arles
Aix-en-Provence
Nice
Èze
Villeneuve-Loubet
Beaulieu-sur-Mer
Mougins
Antibes
Cap d'Antibes
Mediterranean Sea
Cassis
Bandol
Porquerolles
Côte d'Azur

ing more overwhelmingly Provençal than pedaling for miles on end through the lush and perfumed lavender fields surrounding Grignan and its château, once inhabited by prolific letter writer Madame de Sévigné. Let me not forget either those beloved coastal escapes that have often tempted me to trade my island life on Nantucket for a French version on the even smaller island of Porquerolles or one sandwiched into the sunny fishing port of Cassis.

When I'm working as a cycling guide in Provence, I stay with my groups in some of the most beautiful hotels in France. Unfortunately, the visual settings of these hotels frequently surpass what they set out on their dining tables. Luckily, we bicyclists find plenty of time to savor the best of both worlds—fine accommodations and fine regional food—because our cycling routes through the rich Provençal countryside ride like one glorious tour through the dreamiest market in the entire world. We literally inhale the real Provence and taste it in the spontaneous picnics that spring from pedaling through a little village on its designated market day or by serendipitously finding a table or two at an off-the-beaten-path bistro filled with boisterous locals.

As a creative cook, I strive to make recipe resumés of those electrifying tastes of Provence savored during my travels. Inspired as I am by those Impressionist painters who so memorably depicted the South of France, I have found myself infusing my Provençal-derived cooking with a bit of their technique, first making a rough sketch of an appealing image (a flavor in my case) and embellishing it later from memory. Unlike the artist, I don't retreat to some lonely *atelier* to complete and personalize my work; rather, I retreat to my cheerful kitchen and its ocean view on poetic Nantucket Island to find whole new waves of inspiration to be layered upon and fused into my original taste sketches. In this way, the culinary world of my own private Provence has come into recipe being, to be shared with readers in this cookbook.

Henri Matisse insisted that the basis of his art was not intellectual. He once explained: "What I dream of is an art of balance  and purity, of serenity devoid of troubling and depressing subject matter, an art which could be for every mental worker—for the businessman, as well as the man of letters, for example, a soothing calming influence on the mind, something like a good armchair which provides relaxation for physical fatigue." With all due respect to the genius of Matisse, I like metaphorically to think of the lively recipes in this Provençal collection as kindred spirits to his paintings. They tend to be suffused with color, drenched in pure flavors, and titled—sometimes in French, sometimes in English, and once in awhile in Franglais—to seduce with the happiest and most harmonious of sounds. While pedaling through Provence in search of fabulous recipes is undoubtedly incredibly "soothing" and "calming" work, this book is designed to bring joy to both fellow pedalers of Provence and those who simply travel sitting back in the uncomplicated comfort of a good Matisse-style armchair.

# SENSATIONAL
# SPREADS,
# SAUCES,
## AND SIPS OF THE SUN

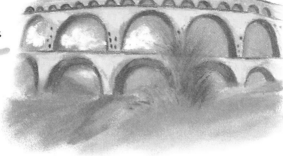

2
...

*Yes, it is true,* one can judge a chef by his sauces. Because it is in a sauce that he reveals himself as a man, a poet, an artist—in brief, a chef. In addition, on any given day his sauce is an expression of a moment, a mood, a state of mind. A mere nothing is sufficient to change the strictest recipe—a thought that occurs, a remembrance of a flower, or of a woman, the bouquet of a wine, the Fragrance of a fruit, or of a truffle, or an herb. . . . In the long run, only a happy chef makes a good sauce.

—Roger Vergé
*Cuisine of the*
*South of France*

just as many a memorable week of bicycling in Provence has begun with a warm-up ride across the miraculous Pont du Gard, a three-tiered Roman aqueduct west of Avignon dating from A.D. 19, many unforgettable meals in Provence build from the richly flavored olive oil-based sauces that anchor its assertive cuisine.

French cooking has always been associated with refined and highly structured sauces, but those unique to this sunny pocket of southern France are far more versatile and accessible to the home cook than the pesky butter-, cream-, and egg-based ones coddled so reverentially throughout the rest of France. In no time at all, flicks of food processors and grindings of pestles against worn mortars make lusty sauces and silky spreads to swoon over. Tapenades, *anchoïades,* and *aïolis* dabbed on toast begin a meal just as stunningly as they complete fare from the grill, garden, or gratin dish. The natural saltiness of base ingredients such as anchovies, olives, capers, chèvre, and dried cod breeds thirsts that are readily slaked with the anise- and herb-infused apéritifs and light and lovely-hued wines favored in this inspired land.

# bLack oLive aNd fig tapeNade

I f I were a playwright rather than a cookbook author, I most certainly would be tempted to turn this olive-speckled section of culinary exploration into a Tapenade Trilogy because my enthusiasm for the "caviar of Provence" could never be confined to either a single play or recipe. Hence the reason for the following three tapenade variations.

In North America, tapenade is practically synonymous with olive purée, but the name actually derives from *tapeno,* the old Provençal dialect for capers—an ingredient unfortunately omitted from many a transplanted tapenade rendition. Since many of the people on my bicycle tours in Provence find the native spread too salty or pungent with anchovy flavor, I always recommend they try this favorite recipe of mine, laced with the dual sweet-ness and crunchiness of brandy-macerated dried figs. Since the recipe never fails to garner rave reviews from tapenade neophytes and aficionados alike, I've come to consider it my signature tape-nade and confess that my refrigerator is rarely without a bowl of it on hand to spread on toasted bread for spur-of-the-moment entertaining and cravings. It is excellent smeared on grilled fish, chicken, and red meat, or dabbed here and there on grilled or roasted vegetables.

If a tight schedule or terrific manicure prevents you from mak-ing the effort to pit the olives the recipe requires, the black olive purée imported from Italy (often labeled *olivada*) and sold in spe-cialty food stores may be substituted with excellent results.

¾ cup dried Black Mission figs, stemmed and diced
¼ cup brandy
½ cup water
6 anchovy fillets, drained
2 tablespoons capers, drained
1 tablespoon imported Dijon mustard
1¼ cups pitted and chopped imported black olives,
   such as Gaeta, Nyons, or Kalamata, or 1 cup
   olive purée
2 tablespoons fresh lemon juice
⅓ cup fruity olive oil
Freshly ground black pepper, to taste
Toasted rounds of French bread, for serving

1. Place the figs, brandy, and water in a small saucepan; bring to a boil and then reduce the heat and simmer until the figs have absorbed most of the liquid, 10 to 12 minutes. Remove from the heat.

2. Place the anchovies, capers, and mustard in a food processor and process to form a paste. Add the olives and figs, along with any remaining liquid and process until very smooth. Add the lemon juice and olive oil and process again until smooth. Season the tapenade with pepper and transfer to a decorative crock or bowl. Cover and refrigerate until ready to use.

3. Serve the tapenade at room temperature, accompanied by toasted rounds of French bread.

ʍɑkeſ ɑbout 2½ cupſ

.5
...

# greeN oLive, ALMoNd, ANd ArMAgNAc tApeNAde

Of all the stalls in the open-air markets that I've visited throughout Provence, one of my favorite is the tapenade cart at the lively Tuesday morning market in Vaison-la-Romaine. There are usually at least eight different blendings of tapenade for sale, and sample tastes of all are hard to resist. This green olive tapenade appeals not only to my adventuresome palate but also to my love of alliterative recipe titles.

At times, when I'm really longing for the South of France and on a tapenade binge, I'll begin an evening of Provençal entertaining by offering guests a bowl of green olive tapenade with at least one if not both of my other tapenade recipes. Add an apéritif of *pastis* and a bouquet of lavender from my garden, and suddenly Provence no longer seems more than 3,000 miles away.

2 cloves garlic, coarsely chopped
⅔ cup slivered almonds, lightly toastd
3 tablespoons capers, drained
6 anchovy fillets, drained
2 cups pitted imported green olives, such as
    Picholine
⅓ cup Armagnac or other brandy
½ cup olive oil
¼ cup slivered fresh basil
Freshly ground black pepper, to taste
Toasted rounds of French bread, for serving

1. Place the garlic, almonds, capers, anchovies, olives, and Armagnac in a food processor and process until the mixture is coarsely ground. With the machine running, slowly pour the olive oil through the feed tube to bind the mixture into a cohesive yet textured spread. Mix in the basil and season the tapenade with pepper. Transfer the tapenade to a decorative crock or bowl, cover, and let mellow in the refrigerator for a few hours before serving.

2. Serve the tapenade at room temperature surrounded by toasted rounds of French bread. Leftover tapenade will keep in the refrigerator for several weeks.

Makes about 3 cups

# OLIVE OIL SAVOIR-FAIRE

In culinary circles, Provence is often referred to as the place where French cooking ceases to be defined by lavish quantities of butter and cream in favor of the hearty and healthful use of local, green-gold olive oil. One need only spend a day cycling in Provence alongside the graceful beauty of its poetically gnarled, silvery green olive groves to be struck with the desire to cook with olive oil all the time.

The recipes in this book call for three different types of olive oil. When *olive oil* is listed in the ingredients, it indicates that a reasonably priced pure or pomace olive oil should be used because the rather bland flavor of these olive oils will not be destroyed or altered when subjected to heat during sautéing. When a recipe calls for *fruity olive oil,* an olive oil with a pronounced olive flavor and rich green or golden color should be used. Depending on place of origin and brand, fruity tasting olive oils may or may not be extra-virgin. Taste rather than labeling should be the determining factor.

*Extra-virgin olive oils* are not only fruity but also exceptionally smooth since by law their acidity must be less than 1 percent. These exquisite oils result from the first cold pressing of the harvest's finest olives and are therefore often quite expensively priced. I call for extra-virgin olive oil where the flavor is of the utmost importance to the dish. Extra-virgin Italian and Spanish oils tend to be more readily available than high quality French oils in the United States. However, if you are in Provence, try to make a point of purchasing a bottle or two of the utterly sublime olive oil pressed at the Cooperative Oleicole de la Vallée des Baux in Maussane-les-Alpilles. The praises of this oil are sung throughout Provence, and olive aficionados in my cycling groups will often bike there for the tours and tastings conducted around the old mill.

# roasted
# eggplant pistounade

This is definitely the most poetically licensed of the three recipes in my Tapenade Trilogy. I justify including it because almost all the ingredients—from the basil, capers, and chick-peas to the roasted eggplant and green olives—are typically Provençal. The wordplay in the title, which combines the Provençal word for basil pesto—*pistou*—with *tapenade,* was lifted from a vendor's canal-side tapenade stall at the ultra-chic Sunday antique and food market in L'Isle-sur-la-Sorgue.

This village is dubbed "the Venice of the Vaucluse," because a network of gurgling canals heightens the already festive aura of its display of decorative arts. Cyclists lucky enough to pedal through L'Isle-sur-la-Sorgue on a Sunday always end up wishing that armoires, rustic picnic tables, and even whole tapenade stalls fit readily on the back of a bike.

Beyond dynamic flavor, much of the allure in this eggplant-anchored tapenade is that the chick-peas impart a body to the dip not normally present in other Mediterranean eggplant-based spreads, such as baba ghanouj.

2 large eggplants, rubbed lightly with olive oil
1 can (15 ounces) chick-peas, drained
¾ cup imported green olives, such as Picholine, pitted
    and coarsely chopped
3 cloves garlic, minced
1 roasted red bell pepper (page 135), seeded and
    coarsely chopped
¼ cup fruity olive oil
2 tablespoons fresh lemon juice
2 tablespoons capers, drained
½ cup rehydrated sun-dried tomato halves (see Note),
    slivered
¼ cup minced fresh parsley
¼ cup slivered fresh basil
Sea or coarse salt and freshly ground black pepper, to taste
Toasted rounds of French bread, for serving

1. Preheat the oven to 400°F. Line a roasting pan with aluminum foil.

2. Prick the oil-rubbed eggplants in several places with the tip of a sharp knife and place them in the prepared roasting pan. Bake, turning occasionally, until the eggplants feel soft when pierced through the center with a knife, 45 to 50 minutes. Let cool, and then halve the eggplants, scoop out the pulp, and discard the skins. Coarsely chop the pulp and set it aside in a mixing bowl.

3. Place the chick-peas, olives, garlic, and roasted pepper in a food processor. Pulse the machine so that all of the ingredients become coarsely chopped. Add the olive oil and lemon juice and pulse briefly to incorporate.

4. Stir the chick-pea mixture into the roasted eggplant pulp. Stir in the capers, sun-dried tomatoes, parsley, and basil. Season with salt and pepper. Transfer the pistounade to a decorative bowl or

crock, cover, and refrigerate for at least 1 hour to let the flavors blend and mellow.

5. When ready to serve, bring the spread to room temperature and accompany it with toasted rounds of French bread.

Makes about 4 cups

Note: To rehydrate sun-dried tomatoes, simmer them in water to cover for 10 minutes, then drain well.

10

# count Austin de croze's anchoïade

before cycling in the fragrant heart of Provence fueled my obsession with the myriad delights of Provençal cooking, I knew how to only make the basic *anchoïade,* or anchovy spread, that serves as a base for my *pissaladière* recipe. During the plea-surable process of researching this book, I began to experiment with newly discovered *anchoïade* variations and soon became an instant fan of fennel *anchoïade* (see page 12), whose unexpected mildness allowed me to enjoy it in straightforward consumption, spread on toast. Such anchovy enlightenment aroused my curiosity about this recipe, discovered in a paperback reprint of Jean-Noël Escudier's cookbook *The Wonderful Food of Provence*. Escudier, who according to Paula Wolfert's introduction was known in France as Monsieur Provence, in turn described Count Austin de Croze as a "celebrated gastronome," who in turn called his version of *anchoïade* a "quintuple Provençal essence." Needless to say, I was sold on the recipe and the following is my slightly modernized and stylized version of this explosive, unusual, and hauntingly delicious spread.

While this *anchoïade* may be served in the usual manner as a spread for toast, I'm especially fond of a dab of it tucked into the crook of a mushroom cap, endive spear, or fennel slice. Another delicious treat may be made by spreading a layer of it on the crusty ends of French bread and leaving them to stand for a few hours. The bread should then be toasted or grilled until fragrant and crispy, and savored warm.

11

18 anchovy fillets, undrained
¼ cup slivered almonds, lightly toasted
¼ cup walnuts, lightly toasted
3 cloves garlic, coarsely chopped
1 shallot, coarsely chopped
5 moist, dried Black Mission figs, stemmed and coarsely chopped
¼ cup minced fresh parsley
¼ cup slivered fresh basil
1 tablespoon minced fresh tarragon, or 1 teaspoon dried
¼ teaspoon hot red pepper flakes
1 tablespoon orange flower water
1 tablespoon pastis, such as Pernod or Ricard
3 tablespoons extra-virgin olive oil
Toasted rounds of French bread, for serving

1. Combine the anchovies, almonds, walnuts, garlic, shallot, figs, parsley, basil, tarragon, and hot red pepper flakes in a food processor and process to form a coarse-textured paste. Add the orange flower water, *pastis,* and olive oil and process again to incorporate. Transfer to a decorative crock or bowl and let the *anchoïade* mellow for at least 1 hour at room temperature, or for several hours, covered, in the refrigerator.

2. Serve the *anchoïade* at room temperature, surrounded by a plate of toast rounds.

Makes about 1½ cups

# fennel Anchoïade

A cursory glance at my collection of favorite Provençal recipes would have anyone convinced that I am an anchovy lover. But, truth be told, I am the first to discard the obligatory garnish of a whole anchovy from a serving of Caesar salad. The fact is that I only like anchovies when they don't taste or look like what they are, and traditional Provençal cooking abounds with recipes in which anchovies impart a hidden, delicious, hard-to-pinpoint complexity. Witness the following variation of *anchoïade*—a gutsy anchovy spread made throughout the Midi, either as an appetizer to be smeared on toast or raw vegetables or as the base for the popular, onion-laden *pissaladière.* Savor with a *pastis* or refreshing glass of chilled rosé.

1 cup slivered skinned almonds, lightly toasted
10 anchovy fillets, drained
1 cup minced fresh fennel bulb
¼ cup fruity olive oil
2 to 3 tablespoons pastis, such as Pernod or Ricard
¼ cup minced fresh mint
Freshly ground black pepper, to taste
Toasted rounds of French bread, for serving

1. Place the almonds, anchovies, and fennel in a food processor and process to form a thick paste. Add the olive oil and *pastis* and continue processing until smooth. Mix in the mint and season with pepper. Transfer to a decorative crock or bowl and let the *anchoïade* mellow for at least 1 hour at room temperature, or for several hours, covered, in the refrigerator.

2. Serve the *anchoïade* at room temperature, surrounded by a plate of the toast rounds.

Makes about 2 cups

13

# Mortar and Pestle Aïoli

꩜

this is the traditional way of making *aïoli* in Provence, and it is the one I make when I'm there without a kitchen but in close proximity to the truly divine olive oil pressed in the old mill in the sleepy little village of Maussane, in the vallée des Baux.

Ever since I've been guiding bicycle trips in the South of France, I've made a point of preparing an *aïoli* picnic feast for my groups. Over the years, I've concocted a mortar's fill of the garlicky elixir in fields fragrant with ripe Cavaillon melons, salons of elegant châteaux, precipices of picturesque, hilltop villages, and even in the pitch dark of a vineyard owner's rustic *grenier* during the torrential rains and subsequent floods that devastated the town of Vaison-la-Romaine in 1992. All were *aïolis* whose pungency could be aromatically remembered—literally!—throughout the remainder of a pedaling afternoon, and in spirit for years to come.

14

> 8 large cloves garlic, peeled
> 1 teaspoon sea or coarse salt
> 2 large egg yolks, at room temperature (see Box, page 189)
> 1½ to 2 cups extra-virgin olive oil, preferably French
> 1 to 2 tablespoons fresh lemon juice

1. In a large mortar, pound the garlic and salt together with the pestle to form a smooth and creamy paste. Add the egg yolks and stir briskly until light and lemony.

2. Slowly begin to drizzle in the olive oil, stirring constantly with the pestle, to make a very thick and rich, golden-green emulsion. Add lemon juice to taste and thin to a slightly looser consistency. It is traditional to serve the *aïoli* directly from the mortar, but if not serving within the hour, store in the refrigerator until ready to use.

Makes about 2 cups

## GARLIC INTOXICATION

Stories are legendary in Provence about the inordinate amounts of garlic different cooks pack into a single batch of *aïoli*—sometimes more than a head per person—but I personally find eight cloves pungently adequate for my crowd when the *aïoli* is slowly and lovingly stirred in a mortar and pestle, using only the finest and richest olive oil, thinned by a mere spritz of lemon juice. The end result is sincerely the best way I know of explaining to my groups why Provence's beloved poet Frédéric Mistral named his journal devoted to preserving his land's customs and traditions *L'Aïoli*. A single dip into the garlicky mortar, and it is at once easy to understand the breathy bonds of which Mistral wrote: "Aïoli intoxicates slightly, saturates the body with warmth and bathes the soul with enthusiasm. . . . Around an *aïoli*, pungent and yellow-orange as a thread of      gold, tell me where you will not find men who recognize      each other as brothers."

# MY favorite Aïoli

this is the recipe for the *aïoli* I always made when I had my food shop on Nantucket during the 1980s and it remains the version I still make most often. It is lighter in its boldness than

traditional Provençal *aïoli* because it has less garlic (though still plenty!) and is made with a combination of vegetable and olive oils rather than all olive oil. The lemon juice also moderates the intensity of the *aïoli*, and the cream-soaked bread base ensures lushness.

1 thick slice day-old French bread
¼ cup heavy (or whipping) cream or
    whole milk
5 or 6 cloves garlic, minced
2 large egg yolks (see Box, page 189)
1 tablespoon imported Dijon mustard
1 cup vegetable oil
¾ cup extra-virgin olive oil
2 to 3 tablespoons fresh lemon juice
Sea or coarse salt and freshly ground
    black pepper, to taste

16
...

1. Trim and discard the crust from the bread and tear the bread into coarse pieces. Combine the bread and cream in a small bowl and let stand for 5 minutes. Gather the bread into a ball and squeeze out as much liquid as possible.

2. Place the bread, garlic, egg yolks, and mustard in a food processor and process until smooth. With the machine running, pour the oils in a thin, steady stream through the feed tube to make a thick emulsion.

3. Season the *aïoli* to taste with lemon juice, salt, and pepper. Transfer to a decorative crock or bowl, cover, and refrigerate until ready to serve. Bring to room temperature before serving.

Makes about 2 cups

# ADDICTIVE
## AÏOLI TOASTS

A s an exciting sort of global fusion cuisine has crept steadily found myself garnering as much culinary inspiration in home restaurants as I do abroad. Case in point are the *aïoli* toasts served as a signature hors d'oeuvre at James O'Shea's (an Irishman!) West Street Grill, in Litchfield, Connecticut. From the moment I swooned over the grill's heavenly Parmesan-laced *aïoli* oozing and bubbling from being broiled on chewy slabs of toasted peasant bread, I knew I had found the world's most fabulous use for finishing up *aïoli*. Inevitably there was always some left from the Provençal feast of the same name—a feast that I relish in stylizing during summer evenings *chez moi* on Nantucket.

Here is how I tend to make my *aïoli* toasts: Fold ¾ cup of a combination of freshly grated Parmesan and Swiss cheeses into 1 cup of leftover *aïoli*. Lightly toast ¾-inch-thick slabs of country bread or sliced thick focaccia and then smear the surface generously with the cheese-laced *aïoli*. Sprinkle with a bit of paprika, arrange on a baking sheet, and let stand for 30 minutes. Broil the *aïoli* toasts a few inches from the heat until lightly browned, puffed, and bubbling. Cut into bite-size, irregular pieces and serve at once with a glass of crisp Provençal white or rosé wine. Sometimes, I'll add a handful of chopped Nyons or Niçois olives and minced parsley to the *aïoli*. More often than not, I find myself turning this irresistible nibble into my entire noon or evening meal. Students in my cooking classes have even suggested *aïoli* toasts for breakfast! Such enthusiasm for garlic makes me all the more enamoured of the saying "Garlic is the ketchup of intellectuals."

# Sweet Potato Aïoli

I started serving this poetically licensed *aïoli* along with bowls of My Favorite Aïoli at the Nantucket *aïoli* dinner parties I host during the summer. Though I've never encountered anything similar to it in Provence, it is laden with the colors and flavors of that sun-scorched region, and many of my guests love the idea of an eggless yet sinfully rich tasting *aïoli*.

2 large sweet potatoes or yams (¾ to 1 pound each)
¾ cup slivered skinned almonds, lightly toasted
5 large cloves garlic, coarsely chopped
1 teaspoon saffron threads
2 tablespoons fresh lemon juice
½ cup extra-virgin olive oil
Pinch of cayenne pepper
Sea or coarse salt and freshly ground black pepper, to taste

1. Preheat the oven to 425°F.

2. Place the sweet potatoes in a small roasting pan and bake until tender, 45 minutes to 1 hour. Let cool until easy to handle.

3. Place the almonds, garlic, and saffron together in a food processor and process until all is finely ground. Halve the sweet potatoes and scoop out the pulp. Add it to the processor and blend until smooth. With the machine running, add the lemon juice and olive oil, pouring them into the feed tube in a thin, steady stream. Season the *aïoli* with cayenne, salt, and pepper. Transfer it to a decorative crock or bowl, cover, and refrigerate until ready to serve.

18

Bring to room temperature before serving. Sweet potato *aïoli* will keep for up to a week in the refrigerator.

Makes 3½ to 4 cups

# traditional rouille

N ow that the fiery, rust-colored condiment to Provençal soups, *rouille,* has become more mainstream, many recipes call for it to be made like a mayonnaise and flavored with garlic and red pepper. But old and traditional Provençal recipes call for thickening *rouille* with bread crumbs rather than egg yolks, and it is this version that I have come to prefer. The only thing I've changed from the original is that I moisten the bread base with white wine rather than water.

Float a toast round—or two or three—topped with this heavenly *rouille* in any *bouillabaisse*-style soup. Then, once you are hooked on its sunny savor, let your imagination run wild. I love *rouille* as a dip or as a binder in a cold seafood salad.

19

2 *slices day-old French bread, 1 inch thick*
¼ *cup dry white wine*
1 *teaspoon saffron threads*
1 *tablespoon hot water*
3 *cloves garlic*
1 *teaspoon sea or coarse salt*
½ *to 1 teaspoon hot red pepper flakes*
¼ *cup fruity olive oil*

1. Tear the bread slices into coarse pieces. Place them in a small, shallow bowl and sprinkle with the wine. Let stand 5 minutes. Meanwhile, combine the saffron and hot water and let soak a few minutes.

2. Place the soaked bread, saffron, garlic, salt, and hot pepper flakes in a food processor and process to make a smooth paste. With the machine running, add the olive oil, pouring it through the feed tube in a thin, steady stream to create a creamy and homogenous purée. Transfer the *rouille* to a decorative crock or bowl and pass as an accompaniment to a Provençal soup. Leftover *rouille* should be stored, covered, in the refrigerator but brought back to room temperature before serving.

Makes about 1 cup

# brandade à L'américaine

I have long been a lover of *brandade*—a hearty and creamy Provençal purée of salt cod, potatoes, garlic, and olive oil, served warm with slices of toasted bread. Salt cod originally became a popular ingredient in the South of France because Norwegian sailors used to trade their preserved catches of cod for olive oil and fresh vegetables in Nice.

Great history aside, I have never been able to get Americans in my cooking classes to embrace *brandade* with much enthusiasm. Exasperated, I finally decided to spike my *brandade* with something that I know almost all Americans adore—shrimp! While I was tinkering, I also ended up adding the sunny flavors of saffron, tarragon, and roasted red pepper to the basic salt cod purée. My new *brandade* made its debut, appropriately enough, during an evening of watching the televised Winter Olympics in Lillehammer, Norway. With apologies to the French and their time-honored culinary traditions, I must report that my American judges/guests found this *brandade* to be a contender for a gold medal.

½ pound boneless salt cod
2 cups milk
½ teaspoon saffron threads
1 large potato
4 large cloves roasted garlic
      (see Note)
¼ cup fruity olive oil
¼ cup heavy (or whipping) cream
2 teaspoons dried tarragon
1 teaspoon grated lemon zest
¾ pound cooked medium shrimp, cut into ½-inch
      dice
½ cup diced roasted red bell pepper (page 135) or
      pimiento
Sea or coarse salt and freshly ground black
      pepper, to taste
3 tablespoons freshly and finely grated Parmesan
      cheese
Toasted rounds of French bread, for serving

21

1. The day before you plan to make the *brandade,* soak the salt

cod in a bowl of cold water. Change the water 4 to 5 times during the course of 24 hours.

2. The following day, drain the cod and place it in a small skillet. Cover it with the milk and scatter the saffron threads over it. Bring the milk to a simmer over medium-low heat and poach the cod until it flakes easily with a fork, about 25 minutes. Drain the cod, reserving ¼ cup of the milk, and flake with a fork.

3. While the cod is cooking, peel the potato, cut it into coarse chunks, and boil it in a saucepan of water until very tender, about 15 minutes.

4. Drain the potato well and immediately transfer it to a mixing bowl. Using an electric mixer, beat the potato until smooth, spooning in the reserved poaching milk from the cod to aid the process. Add the roasted garlic and the poached cod. Continue beating the mixture until it is smooth and fluffy. Beat in the olive oil and cream. Season the *brandade* with the tarragon and lemon zest.

5. Using a spatula, gently fold in the diced shrimp and red pepper. Season with salt and pepper. The *brandade* may be made ahead up to this point and stored, covered, in the refrigerator for up to 3 days.

6. When ready to serve the *brandade,* preheat the oven to 450°F. Spread the *brandade* in a 9-inch gratin dish. Dust the top with the Parmesan cheese. Bake the *brandade* until it is piping hot and the top is lightly crusted, about 15 minutes. Serve at once with toasted rounds of French bread.

ſerveſ 8 aſ aN appetizer

**Note:** To roast individual cloves of garlic, wrap the desired amount of unpeeled cloves loosely in aluminum foil. Place in a toaster oven or regular oven preheated to 350°F, and cook until soft and aromatic, about 25 minutes. Let cool. Squeeze the pulp from the skins, and use as needed.

# double ſALMON rilletteſ

d uring a luxurious off-season overnight stay in Beaulieu-sur-Mer along the Côte d'Azur, I savored these rich salmon *rillettes* while tucked into a cozy corner table in a local restaurant. Since *rillettes*—coarse, rich meat pâtés usually packed into crocks—are traditionally made from duck or pork meat cooked slowly in its own fat, fish-based *rillettes* would seem to offer the promise of a variation lower in fat. *Mais non,* since butter and cream are needed to give these *rillettes* the body and texture of their meat counterparts. Still, salmon *rillettes* seem to embody perfectly the coastal spirit and decadence of the Riviera, so why not serve them when in a Monaco mood?

23

1 can (14¾ ounces) pink salmon
8 tablespoons (1 stick) unsalted butter, at room temperature
½ cup heavy (or whipping) cream
2 tablespoons dry white vermouth
2 tablespoons fresh lemon juice
½ pound thinly sliced smoked salmon, cut
    into julienne strips
2 tablespoons capers, drained
1 bunch scallions, trimmed and minced
½ cup minced fresh dill
Generous pinch of cayenne pepper
Freshly ground white pepper, to taste
Toasted rounds of French bread or crackers, for serving

1. Place the salmon, butter, cream, vermouth, and lemon juice in a food processor and purée until smooth.

2. Add the smoked salmon, capers, scallions, and dill; pulse the machine to incorporate but not purée the new ingredients. Season the *rillettes* with the cayenne and white pepper. Pack into a decorative crock or bowl and refrigerate, covered, overnight to mellow the flavors.

3. Let the *rillettes* stand at room temperature for at least 30 minutes before serving. Surround with the French bread rounds or crackers and serve like a pâté.

Makes about 4 cups

# WArm goAt cHeeſe toAſtſ

this simple yet addictive nibble comes from the Hostellerie de Crillon-le-Brave—one of the most spectacularly sited and designed hotels in all of Provence. Fortunately, this sleepy hill-top hotel, offering splendid relaxation, is run by a friend of mine, who shares recipes—and warm hospitality—readily.

Since it is not customary to serve elaborate hors d'oeuvres in Provence, I'm inclined to serve these toasts with only a bowl of Nyons olives or crock of tapenade as the perfect prelude to a flavorful Provençal meal. The warm, creamy, and herby goat cheese goes exceptionally well with a glass of cool and crisp rosé wine. The warm goat cheese toasts also may be served as an accompaniment to tossed green or mesclun salads.

*8 ounces creamy white goat cheese, at room*
*temperature*
*3 tablespoons extra-virgin olive oil*
*1½ tablespoons minced fresh thyme*
*36 to 40 toasted rounds of French bread*

1. Preheat the oven to 450°F or preheat the broiler.

2. In a small bowl, use a fork to mash together the goat cheese, olive oil, and thyme until smooth. Spread the mixture onto the rounds of French bread, mounding slightly in the center.

3. Place the rounds on baking sheets and slip briefly in the oven or under the broiler until the cheese melts and begins to bubble, 2 to 3 minutes. Let the rounds cool for a minute or so, arrange on a serving tray, and serve warm.

Makes 36 to 40 rounds

25

# LOU CACHAT

Lou cachat is the old Provençal name for an extremely pungent cheese spread made from dried leftover bits of goat cheese remoistened and marinated in a combination of fiery *eau-de-vie,* fruity olive oil, aromatic herbs, and slivered garlic. The recipe is multifunctional because it clears sinuses and senses while making thrifty use of all the odds and ends of Provence's ubiquitous cheese that inevitably accumulate after days or weeks of market-day buying binges in local villages.

*Lou cachat* may be served either as an appetizer or a cheese course following a meal. How long the cheese is allowed to marinate after the initial day depends on one's personal tolerance for strong and smelly but delicious cheeses.

*12 ounces dry, aged goat cheese, coarsely crumbled*
*⅓ cup extra-virgin olive oil*
*½ cup eau-de-vie or brandy*
*3 cloves garlic, peeled and cut into thin slivers*
*1 tablespoon minced fresh thyme, or 1 teaspoon dried*
*1 tablespoon minced fresh rosemary, or 1 teaspoon dried*
*Freshly ground black pepper, to taste*
*Toasted rounds of French, walnut, or olive bread, for serving*

26

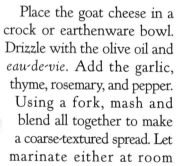

Place the goat cheese in a crock or earthenware bowl. Drizzle with the olive oil and *eau-de-vie*. Add the garlic, thyme, rosemary, and pepper. Using a fork, mash and blend all together to make a coarse-textured spread. Let marinate either at room temperature or covered in the refrigerator for 6 to 12 hours before serving. Serve at room temperature, accompanied by the toasted bread of choice.

Makes about 2½ cups

## FLATS FIXED . . . AND REWARDED

I first tasted *lou cachat* in the less-traveled Haute Var area of Provence while visiting and cycling with friends who had indulged in an autumn vacation rental. One day, I set off on a mid-morning bicycle ride with two sisters from the entourage, both blonde and of Polish descent like myself. After a half-hour or so of riding, one of the sisters got a flat tire. We all stopped, and I expected to resort to my favorite and accustomed way of dealing with flats in France— flirting with local farmers! Unfortunately there were no farmers to be found for miles around. We soon realized that we had no choice but to toil ourselves, long and hard, through most of the lunch hour. By 1:30 P.M., all exposed flesh was smeared with black bicycle grease, and the tire was repaired. Preferring not to be the brunt of jokes back home about how many Polish blondes it takes to change a bicycle tire, we rode on in search of a restaurant and fine meal to reward our pneumatic victory.

Coming upon a tree-shrouded inn at just a hair past 2, I persuaded the chef to take pity enough on three damsels in distress and serve us lunch. He did not have so much pity for us, however, that he would allow us to dine in the company of the well-dressed clientele within. Instead, a table was promptly set up outside in a sunny and secluded private garden, where we feasted long and leisurely on a meal that concluded with the chef's pride and joy— a basket of toasted walnut bread and a crock of *lou cachat,* which, according to the chef, had now been marinating for an incredible *"huit jours!"* Settling the check, we worried not about the possibility of a postprandial flat, for we rose from the table quite assured that breath alone could keep our tires inflated and spirits elated.

27

# provençal tomato sauce

Some may think a tomato sauce is a tomato sauce is a tomato sauce, but I believe in different types of tomato sauce for different types of cuisine. This rich and thick one, simmered with lots of vegetables and whole heads of garlic before it is strained, is the blissful, edible equivalent to the aromatic and rustic countryside through which my cycling groups pedal in Provence. It is based on the recipe from La Mère Besson in film-festival-famed Cannes. Use the sauce on Provençal pastas and pizzas, layered into vegetable *tians*, or as a foil to a towering slice of splendid Crespeou (see Index).

¼ cup fruity olive oil
1 large onion, minced
3 fat leeks, well rinsed, trimmed and minced
3 ribs celery, trimmed and minced
2 carrots, peeled and minced
2 large bulbs garlic, unpeeled, halved horizontally
1½ tablespoons mixed dried Italian herbs
2 cans (28 ounces each) crushed tomatoes in thick purée
½ cup dry red wine
1 to 2 teaspoons sugar
Sea or coarse salt and freshly ground black pepper, to taste

1. Heat the oil over medium-high heat in a large, heavy pot. Add the onion, leeks, celery, carrots, and garlic and sauté until quite soft, 10 to 12 minutes. Add the herbs and sauté for 1 minute more.

2. Add the tomatoes and red wine; bring to a simmer and continue cooking gently, uncovered, stirring occasionally, until thick and very fragrant, 1 to 1½ hours. Let cool until warm to the touch.

3. Pass the sauce through a food mill to purée and strain away the solids and return to a clean pot. Adjust the seasoning with sugar, salt, and pepper. Store in an airtight container in the refrigerator or freeze to be used as needed.

makes about 2 quarts

# garden tomato relish

If Roger Vergé can no longer hold single title to the most famous chef from the South of France, he certainly is, in my opinion, still the most handsome. Since opening the Michelin-rated three-star restaurant Moulin de Mougins along the Riviera in 1969, Vergé has written several cookbooks and consulted on restaurant menus around the world. The recipe below is inspired by one of the first Provençal cookbooks to hit the American market in the late seventies—*Roger Vergé's Cuisine of the South of France.* Vergé noted next to the recipe that it "is an excellent sauce, which one eats a little like a salad with grilled and roasted meats, and with all kinds of barbecue—even fish." I, in fact, pair the sauce most frequently with grilled fish, but I have also served this fresh and colorful vegetable mélange atop toasted bread in the fashion of a Mexican salsa or Italian bruschetta.

5 medium to large vine-ripened tomatoes, seeded
    and diced
1 medium onion, diced
1 red bell pepper, stemmed, seeded, and diced
1 yellow bell pepper, stemmed, seeded, and diced
1 large cucumber, peeled, seeded, and diced
⅓ cup capers, drained
½ cup cornichons, drained and coarsely chopped
2 tablespoons minced fresh tarragon
2 tablespoons slivered fresh basil
½ cup minced fresh parsley
3 tablespoons Champagne vinegar
4 tablespoons imported Dijon mustard
¾ cup extra-virgin olive oil
Sea or coarse salt and freshly ground black pepper,
    to taste

1. In a large earthenware crock or bowl, combine the tomatoes, onion, peppers, and cucumber. Using a wooden spoon, stir in the remaining ingredients, blending well.

2. Cover the relish and let it marinate in a cool but not a cold place (a cellar as opposed to the refrigerator) for 24 hours. Stir the mixture from time to time with a wooden spoon. Serve at room temperature. After 24 hours, leftovers should be stored in the refrigerator but brought back to room temperature before serving.

makes 5 to 6 cups

# PASTIS

*P*astis, a potent apéritif distilled from anise and herbs native to the Mediterranean, is so popular in Provence that it is known as "the milk of Provence." Descended from the lethal and outlawed *absinthe, pastis* is rumored to have gained popularity in the Midi as a cure for a plague that once struck Marseille. France's most popular brand of *pastis,* Ricard, comes from Marseille and is enjoyed at all hours of the day and night.

To truly experience a feeling of oneness with the spirit of place, every visitor to Provence should order a *pastis* at least once while whiling away the hours in an outdoor café. A tall shot glass filled with an inch or so of the licorice elixir will soon arrive with ice and a squat, square carafe of water as accompaniments. An ice cube or two should be plopped into the glass and water added to transform the drink to a cloudy pale yellow and dilute it to a slowly sippable strength. If not immediately enamored, you would be wise to consider taking your vacations elsewhere. On the other hand, if you become a convert, you might just find yourself joining hard-core Frenchmen in their favorite café breakfast—a couple of *pastis* knocked back with several nonfiltered *Gauloise* cigarettes (nutritional analysis not available).

While Pernod tends to be the most widely sold brand of *pastis* in the United States, most bars and liquor stores in Provence stock a handful of different regional labels. Newcomer Henri Bardouin is the current darling of the elite; it has a more herbaceous complexity than many of its competitors and often comes packaged with a logo-imprinted water pitcher and glasses.

*Pastis* is also frequently used in Provençal cooking, especially in fish, rabbit, and poultry dishes, and these days my kitchen is never without an ample supply, lest the plague should return.

31

# apéritif maison, Les domaines

this is the pretty and easy-to-sip apéritif that is the specialty at Les Domaines Wine Bar on the place de l'Horloge in Avignon, the lively city that serves as the rendezvous point for all the cycling trips I lead in Provence. It is the perfect pick-me-up after a morning spent visiting the magnificent nearby Palace of the Popes, and indulging in a second one is apt to make one throw enough care to the wind to be lured for a spin on the fanciful carousel, which twirls to the sound of hurdy-gurdy music day and night on the *place,* just a stone's throw away from the restaurant.

32

6 ounces dry Provençal rosé wine, chilled
2 ounces Muscat de Beaumes-de-Venise, or
    other muscat dessert wine
1 tablespoon framboise liqueur
Ice cubes, optional
1 fresh raspberry (optional), for garnish

Pour the rosé, Muscat, and framboise together into a tall, fluted glass. Add an ice cube, if desired, and garnish with a raspberry, if handy. Sip slowly.

makes 1 cocktail

## L'EAU-DE-VIE DE LONGUE VIE

Mixing all sorts of home-brewed folk libations is a great Provençal pastime. *Recettes en Provence,* the charming, olive-covered cookbook by Andrée Maureau, gives no fewer than sixteen recipes for wines, brandies, and "waters of life," distilled from various fruits, nuts, and herbs. The one that intrigues and amuses me the most is the *eau-de-vie de longue vie.* The maker is instructed to start with a bottle of clear 100- to 120-proof *eau-de-vie* and then spill out a little in order to make room for springs of fresh rosemary, sage, thyme, marjoram, basil, and mint. All is left to macerate for thirty days, after which a few sips a day should be drunk as a surefire formula for living to 100! Hmm . . . I wonder if it discourages wrinkles, too?

33

## viN d'orANge

The more I learn about the mysteries, complexities, and overall wonder of wine, the more I become convinced that I must have a vineyard of my own at some future time. For now, however, I sate my oenological desires by concocting a yearly batch or two of this popular Provençal home brew.

White wine, brandy, and sugar are combined with chunks of fresh orange and lemon and then set to mellow in a cool corner over a period of weeks. The mixture is then strained and further mellowed for a few more weeks before it is ready to be poured—either as a smart apéritif or sweet concluding sip to seal a Provençal feast. It may also be poured over ice, or served with a splash of soda water. *Vin d'Orange* is also quite tasty when poured into the hollow of a really ripe and musky summer melon. And it's not a bad splash to keep stoveside, since it will come in handy now and again—see the recipe for Joie d'Endive!

*4 bottles (750 ml each) dry white wine*
*2½ cups brandy*
*3 to 4 cups sugar*
*5 oranges, scrubbed and then cut into 8 chunks*
*1 lemon, scrubbed and then cut into 8 chunks*

1. Have ready a clean 1- to 2-gallon widemouthed glass jar with a lid. Pour the wine and brandy into it. Add 3 cups of the sugar, stirring with a long wooden spoon to dissolve. Add the orange and lemon chunks. Put the lid on the jar and store in a cool, dark place (such as a cellar) for 5 weeks. It's all right to peek and stir the *Vin d'Orange* from time to time.

2. Strain the mixture and discard the fruit. Taste the wine, and if it seems too astringent, mix in up to 1 cup more of sugar. Return the wine to its cool place and let it age for another week or two before serving. *Vin d'Orange* should be served chilled in small glasses. *Vin d'Orange* keeps for quite a while, though mine rarely lasts long.

Makes approximately 1 gallon

# SOULFUL
# SOUPS

> *FROM TIME IMMEMORIAL,* soups have nourished our
> ancestors and continue to cast a spell over young generations.
> —RICHARD OLNEY QUOTING LULU PEYRAUD
> *LULU'S PROVENÇAL TABLE*

I have bicycled in many pockets of France where the craving for a restorative and energizing bowl of noontime soup has provoked mirages of steaming tureens in the middle of morning routes, for soup as a meal sadly was not considered a part of the region's time-honored traditions. Fortunately, Provence is a soup lover's paradise.

Every local village market looks like a pot of *soupe au pistou* just waiting to be made. The peasant's legendary *aïgo bouïdo* can soothe congestive sniffles as readily as it can a head throbbing from one *pastis* too many the night before. Tomato soup condenses the fragrant essence of a pedal through inland Provence into a bowl, while forays to the coast yield the region's most famous and fantastic soups—*bouillabaisse* and *bourride*. Peter Mayle once said, "Provence is rich in hills, and they all go up," but none of those hills will have been climbed in vain when the gastronomic reward of ladlesful of any one of the memorable soups in this chapter is taken into account.

# poor MAN'S bouiLLAbaisse

$\infty$

*f*or years I've disregarded the fierce battles that rage over how to make a proper *bouillabaisse* and gone my own merry way, making mine with fish that swim in local Cape Cod waters. But for this book, specifically devoted to Provençal food, I feel it only right to heed the famed advice of Fernand Point—*la bouillabaisse* can be made only within sight of the Mediterranean. While we in North America can put together perfectly palatable *bouillabaisse*-style soups, we cannot make an authentic Provençal *bouillabaisse* because we simply don't have access to the sorts of Mediterranean fish that give such sublime character to the Côte d'Azur versions.

Fortunately, there have evolved over the years several poetically licensed forms of *bouillabaisse*. They share the defining characteristic of bringing a broth to a tempestuous boil (*bouillabaisse* literally means to boil and then lower the heat) in order to create a silky liaison between olive oil and broth, though the main ingredient may be as simple as shelled peas, spinach, or sardines.

Of all the variants, I'm most fond of this one, known as a poor man's version because it uses salt cod rather than fresh fish. To my palate it manifests many of the same flavor complexities and riches of its grander, multifish mother. Best of all, Poor Man's *Bouillabaisse* travels, flavor intact, to Atlantic shores, Pacific outposts, and even vast land masses in between.

2 pounds boneless salt cod
⅓ cup fruity olive oil
2 large leeks, well rinsed, trimmed and minced
1 large onion, minced
3 cloves garlic, minced
4 ripe tomatoes, seeded and minced
1 tablespoon grated orange zest
1 teaspoon dried thyme
1 teaspoon saffron threads
¼ cup pastis, such as Pernod or Ricard
10 cups water
2 cups dry white wine
2 pounds potatoes, peeled and
    cut into ½-inch-thick slices,
    larger rounds cut into
    bite-size halves
Sea or coarse salt and
    freshly ground black
    pepper, to taste
1 cup minced fresh parsley
Toasted rounds of French
    bread, for serving
Traditional Rouille
    (page 19), for serving

38

1. The day before you plan to make the *bouillabaisse,* soak the salt cod in a bowl of cold water (this can be done at room temperature), changing the water 4 to 5 times during the course of 24 hours.

2. The following day, heat the olive oil over medium-high heat in a large stockpot. Add the leeks and onion and sauté until quite soft, about 10 minutes. Add the garlic, tomatoes, orange zest, thyme,

saffron, and *pastis* and sauté 5 minutes more. Pour in the water and wine and bring all to a rolling boil. Continue to boil, stirring occasionally, until the oil no longer floats on the surface of the broth but has emulsified with it, 4 to 5 minutes.

3. Add the potatoes, reduce the heat and simmer, until the potatoes are cooked halfway through, 7 to 10 minutes. Meanwhile, drain the salt cod and cut it into 1-inch chunks. Add it to the stockpot and continue simmering until both the potatoes and cod are fully cooked, 7 to 10 minutes more. Season the *bouillabaisse* with salt and pepper; stir in the parsley.

4. To serve the *bouillabaisse,* ladle it into large soup bowls and top each serving with a couple rounds of the toast spread generously with *rouille.* Serve extra toast and *rouille* alongside the *bouillabaisse.*

Makes 8 to 10 servings

*BOUILLABAISSE IS AN INSPIRED CREATION* in which white fish and rockfish, bathed in oil, seasoned with garlic, onions, tomatoes, and herbs, and covered with water, are subjected to a veritable tempest of boiling. Vegetables, herbs, and fishes marry their essences to produce a magic synthesis—the golden bouillon that, powdered with saffron, is at once genial and lusty, velvety and appetizing, reflecting all the dreams and sorcery of the Mediterranean. Bouillon of the sun, savory and substantial, it evokes all the splendor of those shores and the gaiety of their dazzling skies.

—JEAN-NOËL ESCUDIER
*THE WONDERFUL FOOD OF PROVENCE*

# Muffel And Monkfifh bourride

**P**rovençal *bourride* is the lesser known but I think more elegant cousin of *bouillabaisse*. Since the soup is made from species of white fish that also swim in North American waters (cod, halibut, pollack, or monkfish), it can be authentically replicated away from the chic shores of the Côte d'Azur. The soup's exquisite silkiness is produced by whisking garlicky *aïoli* into an already flavorful fish and vegetable broth to form a rich thickening liaison. All is then ladled over the pieces of poached fish and vegetables and garnished with fragrant sprigs of fresh herbs, yielding a truly sublime feast in a bowl.

The *bourride* recipe I offer here is more ornate than some, but it has been created to do poetic justice to the version I slurped and savored to opera arias piped onto the terrace of L'Auberge des Glycines in Porquerolles, after a sunny May day spent biking around the gem of an island.

## MUSSEL BROTH

3 tablespoons olive oil
1 medium onion, minced
6 cloves garlic, minced
1 teaspoon dried thyme
2 teaspoons dried tarragon
1 teaspoon fennel seeds
1½ teaspoons saffron threads
2 bay leaves
1 bottle (750 ml) dry white wine
4 pounds mussels, scrubbed and bearded just before cooking

## BOURRIDE

3 tablespoons olive oil
3 leeks, well rinsed, trimmed and minced
1 carrot, peeled and minced
½ teaspoon saffron threads
4 large potatoes, peeled and cut into ½-inch-thick slices
4 cups water
2 pounds monkfish, membrane removed, cut into
    2-inch chunks
1½ cups cooked fava or butter beans
2 cups aïoli (either My Favorite, page 15, or Mortar and
    Pestle, page 13)
2 large egg yolks
Sea or coarse salt and freshly ground white pepper, to taste

## GARNISHES

2 medium tomatoes, seeded and diced
Small sprigs of fresh tarragon
Small sprigs of fresh basil
Toasted rounds of French bread, for serving

41

1. To make the mussel broth, heat the oil over medium-high heat in a large pot. Add the onion, garlic, thyme, tarragon, fennel seeds, saffron, and bay leaves. Sauté until softened, 5 to 7 minutes. Pour in the wine and add the mussels. Cover the pot, bring to a boil, and continue cooking until the mussels have opened, 5 to 7 minutes. Discard any that haven't opened. When the mussels are cool enough to handle, remove the meats from the shells and discard the shells. (I often save 12 to 16 mussels in the shell for a nice garnish on top of the *bourride.*) Strain the broth through a fine sieve and reserve it, discarding the solids.

2. To make the *bourride,* heat the olive oil over medium-high heat in a large pot. Add the leeks, carrot, and saffron and sauté to soften the vegetables slightly, 5 minutes. Add the potatoes and cover with the water and reserved liquid from the mussels. Bring to a simmer and continue cooking, uncovered, until the potatoes are almost tender, 15 to 20 minutes. Add the monkfish and cook until the pieces are just cooked through, about 5 minutes. Stir in the fava beans and reserved mussel meats and continue cooking a few minutes more to warm through.

3. With a slotted spoon, transfer all the seafood and vegetables to a warmed soup tureen and cover to keep warm. Reduce the heat under the broth to very low.

*IN THE SOUTH OF FRANCE*, "sunny" means you have a light that is nearly three-dimensional, an eye-blinking, chrome-yellow presence that, like a remarkable personality at a party, dominates without trying.

—RICHARD GOODMAN
*FRENCH DIRT*

43

4. Combine 1 cup of the *aïoli* with the egg yolks in a small bowl and whisk until blended. Gradually whisk ½ cup of the hot broth into the *aïoli* and then whisk the mixture back into the broth in the pot, taking care not to let it boil or it will curdle. Continue stirring and cooking over low heat until the broth is creamy and silky-smooth, about 3 minutes. Correct the seasoning with salt and white pepper. Pour the broth over the fish and vegetables in the tureen.

5. To serve, ladle the *bourride* into large, warmed soup plates, making sure everyone gets an ample assortment of the fish and vegetables. Garnish each serving with a scattering of diced tomatoes and a couple of sprigs of the fresh herbs. Tuck a mussel in its shell here and there if you have reserved them. Serve at once and pass the remaining *aïoli* and the toasted French bread separately.

Makes 6 to 8 servings

# ODE TO MY
# MORTAR AND PESTLE

My first mortar and pestle was a small marble one given to me nearly a decade ago by my sister's husband, then a professor of geology at the University of Connecticut. It was the type used in labs at the university, and I used mine in the kitchen only occasionally to grind spices for experimental curries or Caribbean-style "jerked" marinades.

Later, when I began to delve deeply into the traditional methods of Provençal cookery, I realized that all the cooks whom I most respected were singing the praises of puréeing the foundation sauces of their cuisine in a mortar and pestle rather than in a modern food processor. I had only to taste the difference in intensity between a *pistou* mashed slowly in a mortar and pestle compared to one puréed to smithereens by the motorized whirl of a steel food-processor blade to become an instant convert to time-honored ways. I could now appreciate the wisdom in the old Provençal saying that cautions, a proper mortar always smells of garlic.

The foremost order of business on my next trip to the South of France was to purchase a larger mortar and pestle, and I am now the proud owner of a lovely olivewood one, which already smells most fragrantly of garlic. When suitcase space and physical strength allow, I will no doubt someday return home from Provence with the ultimate heavy, white stone mortar and wooden pestle that for me has come to epitomize the lusty essence of the Mediterranean kitchen. In the meantime, after my hands, I would have to declare my olivewood mortar and pestle my favorite culinary gadget and aid. So much for the world of high tech.

# ſoupe au piſtou

~

this vegetable-rich soup, redolent of the basil in a last-minute garnishing spoonful of *pistou*—Provence's pesto—is the stuff of a pedaler's lunch dreams. Indeed, mine were thus fulfilled in a most heavenly manner one midday on the first of what would soon become many visits to Le Bistrot du Paradou.

I was feeling exhilarated after a morning spent climbing from St.-Rémy up the snaking hill that leads to the perched, surreal village of Les Baux and tried to convince a few of my fellow cyclists to join me on a gastronomic side trip that would take us a few kilometers away from our day's route to a lunch-only bistro about which I had recently read terrific reports. My companions understandably wanted to spend their time nosing around the historic attractions of Les Baux or gazing from its rocky perches at the recently biked panorama spilling far and wide below. However, I followed my stomach and biked on alone to what I believe must have been a fated meal.

Flushed from riding in the heat of the high noon sun, I locked my bike in the dusty, nondescript lot that fronted the bistro and then peeked meekly into its cool interior. The restaurant at once struck me as my personal platonic ideal of the quintessential old-fashioned French bistro, with its boisterous crowd, a mix of families, chatty men, and long-married couples seated at dozens of worn marble tables cluttered with white dishes and bottle upon half-drunk bottle of the house red wine. Every single table in the place was taken except the little round one smack in front of me set with a single place. I sat down, and despite being a foreigner and single female diner to boot, I was immediately made to feel like a regular. With a wink of his eye, the proprietor popped

45

the cork on my little table's bottle of red wine and soon brought forth the most delicious *soupe au pistou* I had ever tasted.

Now I don't consider a trip to Provence complete without at least one lunch at Le Bistrot du Paradou and even came to rent a little cottage just up the road from the restaurant while researching this cookbook. *Quelle chance!* It was then that the proprietor jotted down Le Paradou's *soupe au pistou* recipe, which I have used as a guideline for the following transplanted version.

*¼ cup fruity olive oil*
*4 cloves garlic, minced*
*4 leeks, well rinsed, trimmed and minced*
*4 large carrots, peeled and cut into ½-inch dice*
*2 ribs celery, trimmed and sliced on the diagonal into*
  *½-inch pieces*
*½ cup celery leaves, coarsely chopped*
*2 large potatoes, peeled and cut into ½-inch cubes*
*3 cups fresh shell beans such as cranberry or white haricots,*
  *or 2 cans (19 ounces each) white or cannellini beans, drained*
*12 cups water*
*1 can (14½ ounces) diced or stewed tomatoes*
*Sea or coarse salt and freshly ground black pepper, to taste*
*½ pound tender green beans, trimmed and cut into 1-inch lengths*
*1 pound tender young zucchini (2 to 3), trimmed and cut into*
  *⅓-inch dice*
*⅓ pound small pasta, such as ditalini*

PISTOU
*3 cloves garlic*
*1 teaspoon sea or coarse salt*
*2 cups fresh basil*
*⅓ to ½ cup extra-virgin olive oil*
*½ cup freshly grated Parmesan cheese*

1. Heat the fruity olive oil in a large pot over medium-high heat. Add the garlic, leeks, carrots, celery, and celery leaves; sauté until the vegetables just begin to soften, 5 to 7 minutes. Add the potatoes and fresh shell beans, if using. (If using canned beans, add them later with the green beans, zucchini, and pasta.) Cover the vegetables with the water and stir in the tomatoes. Season with salt and pepper. Bring to a boil and simmer, uncovered, stirring occasionally, until the potatoes and beans are tender, 40 to 45 minutes.

2. Add the green beans, zucchini, and pasta and continue simmering the soup until these vegetables are tender and the pasta is al dente, 15 to 20 minutes more.

47

3. Meanwhile, make the *pistou:* Crush the garlic and salt together in a mortar to make a creamy paste. Add the basil, a few leaves at a time, grinding each batch until incorporated into the garlic paste. Slowly work in enough olive oil to thin the *pistou* to a creamlike drizzling consistency. Gently stir in the Parmesan. (Alternatively, though not preferably, all the *pistou* ingredients may be puréed together in a food processor.)

4. Ladle the soup into large bowls and stir a generous tablespoon of *pistou* into each bowl before serving. Extra *pistou* should be passed at the table for those who wish to add more.

Makes 10 to 12 servings

## THE AÏGO BOUÏDO CURE

In Provence, both garlic (*ail*) and sage are considered to be medicinally beneficial, and thus claims about the curative powers of *aïgo bouïdo* abound. The two most popular old Provençal sayings are *"L'aïgo bouïdo sauvo la vido"* (Garlic soup saves life) and *"Qu'a de sauvi dins soun jardin a pas besoun de médecin"* (He who has sage in his garden has no need of doctors). I personally have found a bowl of *aïgo bouïdo* to be equally capable of staving off the common cold and assuaging the foul feelings of a hangover. No mean feat . . . and that is why I have become thoroughly convinced that *aïgo bouïdo* really does cure whatever "ails" one!

# Aïgo biſtro'ſ Aïgo bouïdo

Any Provençal cookbook worth its garlic contains a recipe for this ancient and traditional garlic-laden broth. *Aïgo* is the local slang word for garlic (*ail*), and the recipe for this soup could not be more basic: Simply boil lots of garlic in water flavored with a little olive oil, bay leaf, sage, salt, and pepper. Enrich the broth with either egg yolks or vermicelli and ladle over toasted bread, which may or may not sport a gratinée of Gruyère.

There's only one catch, however, and that is that the best *aïgo bouïdo* I ever tasted was not in Provence but in a bistro located in a train depot in Concord, Massachusetts, conveniently called

Aïgo Bistro. My ecstasy became complete when a phone call to chef Ana Sortun yielded a faxed copy of her sensational recipe within twenty-four hours. Sortun, as it turns out, takes quite a bit of creative license with the original recipe. The garlic is oven-roasted, chicken broth replaces the water, and thickening is achieved by the use of a Spanish *picada*—a mixture of toasted bread crumbs and almonds ground together. The essential peasant nature of the soup is maintained, while the comforting taste and texture is so sublime that I honestly believe I could consume a bowl of *aïgo bouïdo* every day and never tire of it.

The following is my slightly modified version of Ana Sortun's fabulous recipe.

6 tablespoons olive oil
4 heads garlic
Sea or coarse salt and freshly ground black pepper,
    to taste
2 tablespoons unsalted butter
2 large onions, sliced
½ cup heavy (or whipping) cream
10 cups chicken stock, preferably homemade
1 cup dry white wine
1 bay leaf
1 cup whole or slivered almonds, lightly toasted
1¼ cups fresh bread crumbs, toasted
Extra-virgin olive oil and fresh sage sprigs or
    minced parsley, for garnish

1. Preheat the oven to 350°F.
2. Drizzle 4 tablespoons of the olive oil over the bottom of a pie plate or small roasting pan. Slice the garlic heads in half across their width. Sprinkle the exposed surfaces with salt and pepper and

49

place, cut side down, in the prepared pan. Roast until the garlic cloves are very soft and just beginning to caramelize, 25 to 30 minutes. Let cool.

3. Meanwhile, heat the butter and the remaining 2 tablespoons olive oil in a stockpot over medium heat. Add the onions and sauté, stirring frequently, until they turn a pale golden brown, 30 to 40 minutes. Take care not to burn any of the onions.

4. Squeeze the roasted garlic from its skins and discard the skins. Place the garlic and onion in a food processor, add the cream, and purée until smooth. Transfer the mixture to a bowl and set aside. Wash and dry the food processor bowl.

5. Combine the chicken stock, wine, and bay leaf in a clean stockpot. Bring to a gentle boil. Meanwhile, put the almonds and bread crumbs in the food processor and process until very finely ground. Moisten the mixture by ladling 1 cup of the simmering chicken stock into the processor and process again until smooth. Whisk this mixture, along with the garlic-onion purée, into the simmering stock. Stir until well blended and smooth. Correct the seasoning with salt and pepper.

6. Ladle the hot *aïgo bouïdo* into shallow soup bowls. Drizzle a little extra-virgin olive oil over the top of each serving and garnish with either a fresh sage sprig or sprinkling of minced parsley. Serve at once.

Makeſ 6 to 8 ſervingſ

# eggpLANt soup with rouiLLe

If one overlooks southern France's flood-filled autumns of 1992 and 1993, it could almost be said that a day in Provence without eggplant is like a day without sunshine. Eggplant has a chameleon-like ability to carry companion flavors, and the saffron in this hearty soup makes the roasted eggplant and vegetable purée end up tasting strikingly similar to Provence's famed *soupe de poissons*. Hence, I've borrowed the traditional fish soup accompaniments of *rouille*, croutons, and shredded Gruyère cheese to complete the fooling of the palate in this delicious *faux* fish soup.

> 2 medium eggplants, stemmed, peeled in stripes, and then cut into 1-inch cubes
> 2 red bell peppers, stemmed, seeded, and cut into 1-inch-wide wedges
> 3 medium onions, peeled and quartered
> 8 cloves garlic, peeled
> ⅓ cup olive oil
> 2 teaspoons dried oregano
> 1 teaspoon dried rosemary
> ½ teaspoon dried thyme
> 3 ripe tomatoes, quartered and seeded
> 10 cups chicken stock, preferably homemade
> 1 teaspoon saffron threads
> ½ teaspoon hot red pepper flakes
> Sea or coarse salt and freshly ground black pepper, to taste
> Toasted rounds of French bread
> Traditional Rouille (page 19)
> 1 cup shredded Gruyère cheese (4 ounces)

51

1. Preheat the oven to 450°F.

2. Toss the eggplants, peppers, onions, and garlic together in a very large roasting pan. Drizzle with the olive oil, sprinkle with the oregano, rosemary, and thyme, and toss again. Roast the vegetables for 20 minutes, stirring occasionally. Add the tomatoes to the roasting pan and continue roasting and stirring until all the vegetables are very tender and just beginning to char, 30 to 40 minutes more.

3. Transfer the vegetables to a large soup pot and add the chicken stock. Season with the saffron, red pepper flakes, salt, and pepper. Bring the soup to a boil and then simmer, uncovered, to meld the flavors, 30 minutes.

4. Purée the soup in batches in a food processor. Pour into a clean pot and reheat the soup over medium heat. Ladle the hot soup into bowls and accompany with a basket of the toasted French bread rounds and bowls of the *rouille* and shredded Gruyère: Float a couple rounds of bread in each bowl of soup, dollop them with *rouille,* and then sprinkle a little Gruyère over all.

52

Makes 8 to 10 servings

# tomato soup
# aux parfums de provence

One of my favorite French recipe expressions describes a dish as having the *parfums,* or aromatic essences, of either a specific place or mélange of ingredients. This soup is so named because

I created it to recall the intoxicatingly herbaceous scents that waft through the parched September air, which I inhale greedily when cycling through the wild rosemary-and thyme-strewn *garrigues* of the picturesque vallée des Baux.

Originally, I was going to suggest garnishing this bright red soup with either a swirl of contrasting green *pistou* or creamed white goat cheese, but then I discovered that both the presentation and the flavors of the two used in tandem were quite sensational.

> ¼ cup olive oil
> 4 large leeks, well-rinsed, trimmed and minced
> 2 fennel bulbs, trimmed, cored, and minced
> 8 cloves garlic, minced
> 3 carrots, peeled and minced
> ¼ cup minced fresh rosemary
> ¼ cup minced fresh thyme
> 2 tablespoons grated orange zest
> 12 medium vine-ripened tomatoes, seeded and cut into
>       ½-inch dice
> 1 cup dry white wine
> 4 cups chicken stock, preferably homemade, or water
> Sea or coarse salt and freshly ground black pepper,
>       to taste
> Pistou (page 46 and Step 3, page 47)

> CREAMED GOAT CHEESE
> 4 ounces creamy white goat cheese
> ⅓ cup heavy (or whipping) cream

1. Heat the olive oil in a large pot over medium-high heat. Add the leeks, fennel, garlic, carrots, rosemary, thyme, and orange zest;

53

sauté until the vegetables are quite soft, 15 to 20 minutes. Add the tomatoes, wine, and stock or water; season with salt and pepper. Bring the soup to a boil and then simmer, uncovered, stirring occasionally, for 45 minutes.

2. Meanwhile, make the *pistou*. Then make the goat cheese cream: Place the goat cheese and cream in a food processor and purée until smooth. Transfer to a bowl and set aside briefly.

3. To finish the soup, purée half of it in a blender or food processor, and then recombine it with the original mixture in the pot. If the soup has cooled, reheat it over low heat. Ladle the hot soup into serving bowls and drizzle the top of each serving with 1 tablespoon each *pistou* and creamed goat cheese. Using the tip of a knife, swirl the two toppings together to create a marbleized pattern. Serve at once.

Makes 6 to 8 servings

# Harvest Soupe d'épeautre

*epeautre* is an ancient strain of wild wheat that grows in the plains around the town of Sault, east of Mont Ventoux. The golden grain manages to taste simultaneously sweet, nutty, and crunchy, and I have become so enamored of it that I make it a priority to bring a few bags of *épeautre* back from Provence on every trip. If, however, you find yourself *épeautre*-less in North

America, whole wheat berries make a reasonable substitute, though they tend to be slightly tougher and chewier and require soaking before cooking.

Risotto d'épeautre is the current rage in fashionable Provençal restaurants, but the most traditional use for the grain has long been this hearty peasant soup, usually prepared to celebrate the wheat harvest around the time of the autumnal equinox. The thick, textural soup is stick-to-your-ribs fare of the first order, and whenever I make a batch I imagine myself transported to a cozy corner of a rustic, Provençal *mas,* safe from the awesome *mistral* wind howling fiercely down the Rhône valley.

Since lamb is the meat most favored in Provençal cooking, I usually make lamb stock from the bones inevitably left from many a Provençal feast, but beef stock may also be used in this recipe. Merguez is a spicy lamb sausage of North African origin that is popular in the South of France. It is available in specialty meat markets in the United States, but you may also feel free to substitute a spicy Italian or Spanish sausage in its place. In other words, please don't let the perceived esoterica of a few of the ingredients in *soupe d'épeautre* discourage you from undertaking the preparation of this uniquely wonderful meal. Accompany it with bread and a simple salad.

3 tablespoons olive oil
1 pound lean ground lamb
1 large onion, minced
5 cloves garlic, minced
3 carrots, peeled and cut into ½-inch dice
2 ribs celery, trimmed and cut into ½-inch slices
1½ cups épeautre, rinsed, or 1½ cups whole wheat berries,
    soaked in cold water to cover overnight
8 to 10 cups lamb or beef stock
1 cup dry red wine
Sea or coarse salt and freshly ground black pepper, to taste
1½ cups cubed (¾ inch) winter squash or sweet potato
1 pound merguez sausage links, or other spicy link sausage
½ cup minced fresh parsley

1. Heat the olive oil in a large pot over medium-high heat. Add the lamb and cook, crumbling it into bits with the back of a wooden spoon, until it loses its pink color, 5 to 7 minutes. Add the onion, garlic, carrots, and celery and continue cooking, stirring frequently, until the vegetables are softened, 10 to 12 minutes.

2. Add the *épeautre* or drained wheat berries and pour in 8 cups of the stock and the red wine. Season with salt and pepper. Simmer the soup, uncovered, until the grains are tender but still slightly chewy, 45 minutes to 1 hour. Add more stock if the mixture is becoming very thick.

3. Add the diced squash or sweet potato to the soup and continue simmering until it becomes tender, 25 to 30 minutes.

4. Meanwhile, cut the sausage links on the diagonal into ½-inch slices. Brown in a skillet over medium heat, turning to crisp both sides, about 10 minutes total. Stir the sausage and parsley into the soup and ladle hearty portions into big soup bowls.

Makes 6 servings

# PROVENÇAL
# PASTAS,
# PIZZAS,
## AND SUNDRY SAVORIES

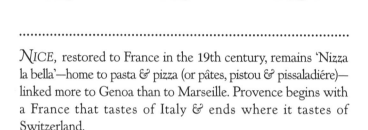

*NICE,* restored to France in the 19th century, remains 'Nizza la bella'—home to pasta & pizza (or pâtes, pistou & pissaladiére)— linked more to Genoa than to Marseille. Provence begins with a France that tastes of Italy & ends where it tastes of Switzerland.

—LESLIE FORBES
*A TASTE OF PROVENCE*

I can still vividly remember my first trip to the heart of Provence. I had been in Burgundy for the previous two and a half weeks, bicycling and eating the traditional, rich, multicourse meals of the region. As I sped down the Autoroute du Soleil past Valence and on toward Avignon, I had lazing in warmth and sunshine on my mind, not partaking of more elaborate dinners. Arriving in Avignon in the early afternoon, I sat myself down at the sunniest sidewalk table on the colorful, pedestrians-only place de l'Horloge. I ordered a cool drink and a simple piece of pizza, whose intense purity of perfectly flavored tomatoes and parsley made me sit up and take culinary notice. It had been weeks since I had tasted such sun-drenched flavors or had been allowed to order anything as frivolous as a piece of pizza in a French restaurant!

Such was my delightful introduction to *la dolce vita*—the Italian influence on Provençal cuisine. Subsequent bicycling expeditions to the South of France have brought me my fill of uniquely Provençal pastas, pizzas, breads, sandwiches, and omelets. Not only are these specialties highly compatible with cravings developed while pedaling through Provence, they also appeal to the way I love to cook and eat once I'm back home blissfully recreating all the inspiring new tastes of my memorable travels.

# pâtes au pistou

P*âtes au pistou* (pasta with pesto) is as fun to say in French as it is to consume. Most Provençal food lovers rave about the creamy version served at the hole-in-the-wall restaurant La Merenda, in Nice, but I'm crazy for the tomato-speckled helpings dished forth at the bustling Bistrot des Alpilles in St.-Rémy.

While St.-Rémy certainly boasts many charming and good restaurants, Le Bistrot des Alpilles is a perennial favorite of locals and participants on my bike trips alike. Despite the fact that the restaurant proudly advertises its founding in 1984, its deep cyprus-green walls dotted with old photographs, tables covered with Provençal mustard-colored printed fabric, and tomato-red awning make it look as if it has been an integral part of the Provençal landscape forever. Classic good food at the bistro ranges from *artichauts à la barigoule* to *gigot d'agneau* to *salade verte au chèvre chaud,* but still I can never resist twirling my fork deep into a basil-inundated bowl of the exceptional *pâtes au pistou*—which makes me especially glad that I persisted in begging the Moroccan-born chef for his recipe.

5 medium ripe tomatoes, peeled, seeded, and diced
¾ cup shredded fresh basil
6 cloves garlic, minced
¾ cup minced fresh parsley
½ cup extra-virgin olive oil
1½ teaspoons herbes de Provence
Sea or coarse salt and freshly
    ground black pepper, to taste
1 pound fresh fettuccine or
    tagliatelle
3 tablespoons unsalted butter,
    at room temperature
Freshly grated Parmesan cheese, for serving

1. Combine the tomatoes, basil, garlic, and parsley in a medium-size bowl. Toss with the olive oil, *herbes de Provence,* salt, and pepper. Let stand at room temperature for at least 30 minutes.

2. Bring a large pot of salted water to a boil and cook the pasta just until tender, about 3 minutes. Drain and immediately toss the hot pasta with the butter. Once the butter has melted, divide the pasta among 4 to 6 serving plates and top each generously with a portion of the tomato-basil mixture. Serve at once with a side of freshly grated Parmesan cheese.

Makes 4 to 6 servings

# Spaghetti with Anchovies and Lemon Zest

**C**ycling-induced carbohydrate cravings aside, this is the sort of easily executed pasta dish that I could be perfectly happy eating once a week. As with so many of the recipes in this book that call for anchovies, the anchovies impart an underlying complexity and depth of flavor that will not be readily recognizable as the taste of anchovy in the end result.

Many Provençal cuisine purists insist that anchovies preserved in salt be used in their recipes and that anchovies canned in oil are by no means a comparable substitute. Salt-packed anchovies are sold in some ethnic markets in North America, and I have experimented with ones I smuggled back from Provence. Admittedly, the flavor of the salted anchovies is superior, but not so superior that I would discourage the use of canned anchovies. Generally, even after rinsing, salted anchovies taste stronger than canned ones and are therefore used in lesser quantities.

61

4 salt-packed anchovies, rinsed and filleted, or 10 oil-packed
    anchovy fillets, drained
4 tablespoons (½ stick) unsalted butter, at room temperature
5 tablespoons fruity olive oil
1 large, ripe beefsteak tomato, seeded and diced
4 cloves garlic, minced
½ cup minced fresh parsley
1 tablespoon grated lemon zest
Freshly ground black pepper, to taste
¾ pound spaghetti

1. Finely mince the anchovies, and using a fork, mash them into the butter in a small bowl until thoroughly combined. Set aside.

2. Heat the olive oil in a medium-size skillet over medium-high heat. Add the tomato and sauté until its juices have begun to reduce and thicken, 5 to 7 minutes. Add the garlic and continue sautéing until it is softened and mellowed, 3 minutes more. Stir in the parsley and lemon zest; season with pepper and keep warm over very low heat.

3. Meanwhile cook the spaghetti in a large pot of boiling, salted water until *al dente*; drain. Immediately toss the hot spaghetti with the mashed anchovy butter until all of the strands are coated. Toss with the tomato sauce and serve at once.

makes 4 servings

# fisherman's fettuccine alla carbonara

⌣

I tend to retain especially vivid memories of the first dishes I sample when arriving at a foreign destination. Having Nice (or "The Big Olive," as the locals call it) as my gateway to travels in Provence always puts me in the best of moods, but digging, fresh off the plane, into a bowl of *carbonara du pêcheur* in one of the pretty, patioed restaurants that dot Vieux Nice doesn't hurt, either. The recipe shows how adept the Niçois are at marrying neighboring Italian influences on the city's cuisine with their own local seaside bounty.

½ pound pancetta, cut into ½-inch dice

2 large onions, cut into crescent-shaped slivers

1 pound cleaned calamari, tentacles left whole and bodies
   cut into ½-inch-wide rings

½ pound sliced smoked salmon, cut into ½-inch-wide strips

2 teaspoons grated lemon zest

½ cup minced fresh parsley

5 whole eggs, at room temperature

1 cup heavy (or whipping) cream, at room temperature

Freshly ground black pepper, to taste

1½ pounds fettuccine

1. Heat a large skillet over medium-high heat and add the pancetta. Cook, turning frequently, until browned and crisped all over, 8 to 10 minutes. Using a slotted spatula, transfer the pancetta to a plate lined with paper towels to drain.

2. Add the onions to the fat remaining in the skillet and sauté them over medium heat until golden brown, 20 to 25 minutes. Stir in the calamari tentacles and rings and cook for 1 minute. Add the smoked salmon and lemon zest and continue cooking until the calamari is just cooked through, 1 to 2 minutes more. Add the parsley and keep warm over the lowest possible heat.

3. Beat the eggs and cream together in a large bowl. Season generously with pepper. (I generally don't add salt, since both the pancetta and smoked salmon add enough salt to the finished dish for my tastes.)

4. Meanwhile, cook the fettuccine until *al dente* in a large pot of boiling salted water. Drain and immediately toss the hot pasta with the egg and cream mixture so the pasta cooks the eggs. Mix in the onion-seafood mixture and the cooked pancetta, tossing until all is evenly distributed. Serve at once.

Makes 6 to 8 servings

# pissaladière

before I developed a passion for Provence, I had a cherished *pissaladière* recipe that I made daily in my food shop on Nantucket and marketed as French Onion Tart. It was extremely popular, and most of my customers never imagined that much of its lusty flavor came from a layer of *anchoïade*—or anchovy spread—sandwiched in between the pizza-dough crust and the lavish sautéed onion topping. In Nice, I came to learn that this onion pizza is so beloved that old-timers sing a song about astronauts landing on the moon and discovering "the sweetest smell in the world" coming from three Niçois already there and lunching on *pissaladière*. I also discovered that I preferred my version of *pissaladière* to any I sampled along the Côte d'Azur, where the crust is frequently oily pastry rather than spongy yeasted dough and the anchovies are usually pungently criss-crossed over the top of the onions rather than muted in a purée and spread underneath.

64

Here is my original recipe; I recommend packing it for one of "the sweetest smelling" Provençal picnics imaginable. Leftovers, by the way, make a smart hors d'oeuvre when cut into bite-size squares.

*Pizza Dough (recipe follows)*

ANCHOÏADE
4 tablespoons anchovy paste
2 large cloves garlic, minced
1 tablespoon balsamic vinegar
½ cup minced fresh parsley
½ teaspoon dried thyme
1 large egg yolk
½ cup fresh white bread crumbs
½ cup olive oil
Freshly ground black pepper, to taste
1 to 2 tablespoons fresh lemon juice

ONION TOPPING
3 tablespoons fruity olive oil
4 very large Spanish onions, thinly sliced
1 tablespoon sugar
2 cloves garlic, finely minced

65

Cornmeal for sprinkling on the baking pan
Niçois or Nyons olives, for garnishing

1. Make the pizza dough.

2. While the dough is rising, make the *anchoïade*: Place the anchovy paste, garlic, vinegar, parsley, and thyme in a food processor and process to a smooth paste. Add the egg yolk and bread crumbs and process again until smooth. With the machine running, pour the oil through the feed tube in a thin, steady stream to make a smooth and thick emulsion. Season with the pepper and lemon juice.

3. Prepare the onion topping: Heat the oil in a very large skillet over medium-high heat. Add the onions and cook, stirring frequently,

until they are quite soft, about 15 minutes. Reduce the heat to medium and continue to cook, stirring frequently, for another 10 minutes. Stir in the sugar and raise the heat to caramelize the onions, cooking and stirring for 5 to 7 minutes more. Add the garlic and cook until it is softened and mellowed, 2 minutes more. Remove from the heat.

4. Preheat the oven to 375°F. Lightly sprinkle a 15 × 12-inch low-sided baking sheet with cornmeal.

5. Punch down the pizza dough and roll it out on a lightly floured surface to a rectangle slightly larger than the prepared baking sheet. Transfer the dough to the sheet pan and trim and crimp the edges decoratively.

6. Spread the *anchoïade* evenly over the surface of the pizza dough. Top with all of the onions spread in an even layer.

7. Bake the *pissaladière* until the crust edges are golden and the onions have turned an even richer golden brown, 40 to 45 minutes. Let cool to room temperature. Cut into serving pieces and garnish each with an olive or two.

Serves 6 to 8 as a pizza or 15 to 20 as an Hors d'oeuvre

# pizza dough

1⅔ cups warm water (105 °F to 115 °F)
2 teaspoons active dry yeast
1 teaspoon sea or coarse salt
1½ tablespoons fruity olive oil
½ cup whole-wheat or rye flour
3 to 4 cups bread flour

1. Pour the warm water in a large mixing bowl. Sprinkle the yeast over the water and mix it in by swirling the bowl until the water turns creamy. Let sit for 5 minutes. Stir in the salt and oil and then the whole-wheat or rye flour to make a sticky batter. Using a wooden spoon, gradually stir in enough of the bread flour to make a moderately stiff dough.

2. Turn out onto a lightly floured surface and knead until smooth and satiny, 5 to 7 minutes. Place dough in a clean, large bowl, cover tightly with plastic wrap or a tea towel, and let rise in a warm spot until doubled in bulk, about 1½ hours. Then use the dough as directed in a main recipe.

ENOUGH dough for a 15 × 12-inch pizza

67

# pizza
# de La pluie

Yes, *la pluie* (rain) does exist in the sunny South of France, and, truth be told, Provence has had more than its fair share of wetness in the last couple of years. In 1993, I spent almost an entire September week in the rain in the Var. Friends who had previously shared weeks of great weather, wining, dining, and exercising on Butterfield & Robinson trips I had led over the years, invited me to join them in a rental villa for what was to be a week of cycling in untouristed hill towns of Haute Provence and cooking at home. The terrain of these hill towns ended up being formidable and the rain relentless, but the cooking at La Tuilerie, our stone abode that had been converted from a ceramics workshop into a sprawling, open-beamed house, turned out to be terrific.

I seized the occasion for recipe feedback by making many of the dishes I intended to include in this book. On the day before I was to leave, the weather broke, allowing me to savor one fabulous bike ride through fields of late-blooming lavender to the quaint village of Moustiers-Ste.-Marie, known for its pretty pastel pottery. The rain, however, soon returned, and I was back in the blue-tiled kitchen, hungry and trying to do something creative and satisfying with all the wonderful little its and bits of Provençal leftovers that had accumulated during the week. Pizza de la Pluie was thus born.

*Cornmeal for sprinkling on the baking pan*
*Pizza Dough (page 66)*
*½ cup Count Austin de Croze's Anchoïade (page 10) or*
    *Fennel Anchoïade (page 12)*
*½ cup Black Olive and Fig Tapenade (page 3)*
*3 medium ripe tomatoes, thinly sliced*
*6 ounces thinly sliced cooked leg of lamb*
*4 fresh figs or 8 dried ones, quartered*
*6 ounces blue or goat cheese, crumbled*
*4 ounces melting cheese, such as Gruyère or*
    *mozzarella, shredded*
*1 tablespoon herbes de Provence*
*2½ tablespoons fruity olive oil*

1. Preheat the oven to 400°F. Lightly sprinkle a 15 × 12-inch low-sided baking sheet with cornmeal.

2. Punch down the pizza dough, roll it out on a lightly floured

surface to a rectangle slightly larger than the prepared baking sheet. Transfer the dough to the sheet pan and trim and crimp the edges.

3. Spread the *anchoïade* and tapenade together over the surface of the pizza dough, swirling it with a knife to create a marbleized effect. Arrange the tomato slices, lamb slices, and fig quarters randomly over the pizza. Sprinkle evenly with the crumbled blue or goat cheese, shredded melting cheese, and *herbes de Provence*. Drizzle with the olive oil.

4. Bake the pizza until the cheese is bubbling and the crust is golden, 30 to 40 minutes. Serve hot or warm, cut into large squares.

Makes 6 servings

69

# bLack oLive aNd swiss chard tart

As much as I love the bold and distinctive style of Niçois cooking, I have never been able to muster much fondness for the *tarte de blettes*—a sweetened Swiss chard and raisin quiche— sold in almost all the food shops of Vieux Nice. Then I came across this savory version, in which black olives take the place of the raisins, and it was love at first and last bite. Serve the tart accompanied by a mesclun salad for lunch, or begin a more formal Provençal dinner with a warm and dainty wedge. The rich complexity of a white Châteauneuf-du-Pape wine would make a lovely marriage.

PASTRY

1¼ cups unbleached all-purpose flour

1½ tablespoons minced fresh rosemary

Pinch of sea or coarse salt

8 tablespoons (1 stick) chilled unsalted butter, cut
    into small pieces

2 teaspoons imported Dijon mustard

2 to 3 tablespoons ice water

FILLING

1 large bunch Swiss chard (about 1 pound), washed, stems
    and thick center ribs removed, leaves patted dry

2 tablespoons olive oil

1 large onion, minced

3 cloves garlic, minced

½ teaspoon dried thyme

Pinch of grated nutmeg

½ cup freshly grated Gruyère cheese

2 large eggs

½ cup light cream or half-and-half

Sea or coarse salt and freshly ground black pepper,
    to taste

2 cups pitted Nyons or Kalamata olives

2 tablespoons pine nuts

1. Make the pastry: Place the flour, rosemary, salt, and butter in a food processor and pulse until the mixture resembles coarse meal. Add the mustard and enough ice water so that the dough begins to form a ball as the machine is pulsed on and off. Gather the dough into a flat disk, wrap it in plastic, and refrigerate for at least 30 minutes.

2. Meanwhile, make the filling. Cut the Swiss chard leaves into ½-inch-wide strips. Heat the olive oil in a large skillet over medium-high heat. Add the onion and sauté until soft and  translucent, 7 to 10 minutes. Add the chard, garlic, thyme, and nutmeg. Cook until the chard leaves have wilted and any water given off has evaporated, 5 to 7 minutes. Remove from the heat and gently mix in the cheese.

3. Beat the eggs and cream together in a mixing bowl and then fold in the chard mixture, blending well. Season with salt and pepper and set aside.

4. Preheat the oven to 400°F.

5. On a lightly floured surface, roll out the chilled pastry dough to form a 12- to 13-inch circle. Transfer to an 11-inch tart pan and trim and crimp the edges decoratively. Spread the chard filling evenly in the tart shell. Arrange the olives in concentric circles over the top, pressing lightly into the filling. Sprinkle the pine nuts in between the olives.

6. Bake the tart until the crust is golden and the filling is set, 30 to 40 minutes. Serve hot, warm, or at room temperature.

ſerveſ 6 to 8 aſ a LUNCHeon or 12 to 14 aſ an appetizer

71

# I LOVE OLIVES

*THE WHOLE MEDITERRANEAN,* the sculpture, the palms, the gold beads, the bearded heroes, the wine, the ideas, the ships, the moonlight, the winged gorgons, the bronze men, the philosophers, all of it seems to rise in the sour, pungent taste of these black olives between the teeth. A taste older than meat, older than wine. A taste as old as cold water.

—LAWRENCE DURRELL

The arid yet fragrant Provençal landscapes of gnarly, silver-green olive groves that we meander through on bicycles serve as a preview to a cuisine rich in olive and olive oil recipes. There are three main olives that come from Provence: Niçois, Nyons, and Picholine. Niçois olives are the smallest and sport an enticing purplish black sheen; since they are the most masochistic to pit, they are favored for serving in bowls as an hors d'oeuvre or using whole in recipes.

Nyons olives from northern Provence are a true connoisseur's olive, for they are plump and meaty, and the smooth and slightly smoky flavor of their flesh is usually enhanced by a marinade of olive oil, garlic, and *herbes de Provence.* Nyons olives are great for both cooking and eating, and when a bicycle route in Provence takes us to the olive museum and Cooperative Agricole du Nyonsais, I always recommend that my group buy the easily packed plastic pouches of local olives for gifts and souvenirs. For those who read French, the cooperative also sells a good little book of olive cookery called *Les Olives du Soleil dans la Cuisine,* by Simone Chamoux.

Picholine olives are probably my favorite green olive; they are a graceful, pointy oval shape and have a sweet yet crisp flesh. Since they are fairly easy to pit, they are my choice for use in making green-olive tapenades. Green *olives cassées* are a celebrated autumn specialty in Provence. They are made from the season's first-harvested olives, which are individually cracked with a mallet to break and bruise the flesh before being marinated in an herbaceous brine for ten days to two weeks. *Olives cassées* are firm with a fresh, grassy, and slightly bitter flavor.

The recipes in this book call for Provençal olives along with unspecified types of imported olives. A general rule of thumb is that the larger the olive, the easier it is to pit and the more flesh it yields for the least amount of work. For this reason, I will often use Greek Kalamata and Alfonso olives or Italian Gaeta olives in recipes that require pitting. These olives are also more readily available than Provençal olives in many markets around the country. Do not cheat with canned prepitted olives labeled "black ripe" from California, for they have no flavor. Many ethnic and specialty stores now offer a virtual Mediterranean pantry of barrels of olives prepared in innumerable ways. Whenever I can, I will stock up on such irresistible olive assortments because my travels in Provence have turned me into an olive addict who wants to believe that peace and harmony at the table or in a recipe just might begin with an offering of excellent olives.

# pain provençal

༼

**t**his focaccia-like flatbread is speckled with many of the rich and warm Provençal flavors I have come to adore. Apparently, many of my friends must have the same taste, because the bread never fails to garner rave reviews. Since it is relatively easy to make, I often find myself offering it solo, as a nibble to temper the potent effects of rounds of *pastis* or other choice libations. *Pain Provençal* is also welcome tucked into a lunch or dinner bread basket. If you don't have access to untreated lavender blossoms, double the amount of rosemary or use 2 tablespoons dried *herbes de Provence* as a substitute for both herbs.

¾ *cup warm water (105 °F to 115 °F)*
1 *package (2½ teaspoons) active dry yeast*
¼ *cup plus 2 tablespoons fruity olive oil*
2½ *to 3 cups bread flour*
½ *cup imported black olives, pitted and coarsely chopped*
1½ *tablespoons fresh or dried untreated lavender*
    *blossoms*
1½ *tablespoons fresh rosemary, coarsely chopped*
½ *tablespoon sea or coarse salt*

1. Pour the water into a large mixing bowl. Sprinkle the yeast over the water and mix it in by swirling the bowl until the water turns creamy. Let proof for 5 minutes. Using a wooden spoon, stir in ¼ cup of the olive oil and 1 cup of the flour to make a very sticky dough. Mix in the olives and two-thirds each of the lavender and rosemary. Gradually work in enough of the remaining flour to make a smooth dough that no longer sticks to the sides of the bowl. Turn

out the dough onto a lightly floured surface and knead until very smooth and elastic, 5 to 7 minutes.

2. Transfer the dough to a clean bowl, cover tightly with plastic wrap or a tea towel, and set in a warm spot to rise until doubled in bulk, about 1 hour.

3. Preheat the oven to 425°F. Line a 15 × 10-inch jelly-roll pan or baking sheet with parchment paper.

4. Punch down the dough and turn out onto a lightly floured surface. Roll out into a rectangle measuring approximately 14 × 9 inches. Transfer to the prepared baking sheet and let rest for 20 minutes. Press the surface of the dough all over with your fingertips to create indentations. Brush the top with the remaining 2 tablespoons olive oil and then sprinkle evenly with the remaining herbs and the salt.

5. Bake the bread until puffed and light golden brown, about 20 minutes. Serve the bread warm or at room temperature, cut into any shape that pleases you.

Makes 8 to 10 servings

# fougasse aux grattons

*f*ougasse is the favorite flatbread of Provence. The bread is often shaped into large, leaflike disks and then slashed on the diagonal in several places to create a distinctive, lacy pattern.

The pizzalike dough may be flavored with olives, anchovies, cheese, walnuts, or my favorite, *grattons*—crispy fried pork or duck cracklings. The truth is that I'm so enamored of *fougasse aux grattons* that I've been known to skip the standard French *petit déjeuner* of *café au lait* and croissants in favor of tucking a just-baked, warm *fougasse* from a local bakery into my front bike pack to fuel a morning of hilly biking about the Luberon or Alpilles. Quite the unique and enjoyable way of focusing on a "balanced" diet!

Reproducing the sinful qualities of Provençal *fougasse* in the home kitchen requires some effort. But, if you are as driven by cravings and the quest for perfection as I am, you'll probably be willing to muster the patience to make the dough's starter, seek out the proper flour, and not wince too much when mixing a half-pound of crisped bacon along with all of its rendered fat into the dough after its first rising. While a perfectly adequate dough may be made using the bread flour sold in most supermarkets, superior results that most closely resemble a French *fougasse* may be achieved by using King Arthur's newly developed American "French" flour (available by mail-order only, in 5-pound bags; phone 800-827-6836).

STARTER
¼ cup warm water (105 °F to 115 °F)
½ teaspoon active dry yeast
1¼ cups room-temperature water
3 cups King Arthur American "French" flour
    or other bread flour

DOUGH
1¼ cups warm water (105 °F to 115 °F)
1 teaspoon active dry yeast
2 tablespoons olive oil
½ cup rye flour
1½ teaspoons sea or coarse salt
3 to 3½ cups King Arthur American "French" flour or
    other bread flour
½ pound double-smoked slab bacon, rind discarded, cut
    into ¼-inch dice
1 large egg beaten with 1 tablespoon water

1. Early in the day or on the day before you plan to bake, make the starter: Pour the warm water into a large mixing bowl. Sprinkle the yeast over the water and mix it in by swirling the bowl around until the water turns creamy. Let stand until foamy, 5 minutes. Using a wooden spoon, stir in the room-temperature water and then the flour to make a smooth and heavy batter. Cover the bowl tightly with plastic wrap and let rise in a cool place for at least 6 hours, but no longer than 24 hours.

2. To make the *fougasse* dough, pour the warm water into a large mixing bowl. Sprinkle the yeast over the water and swirl the bowl until the water turns creamy. Let stand until foamy, 5 minutes. Stir in the olive oil, rye flour, and salt. Now add about two-thirds of the starter after separating it from the rest with your hands or a

knife (the remaining starter may either be saved to add to sourdough bread or discarded). Using a wooden spoon, stir vigorously to incorporate it into the mixture. Gradually work in enough of the "French" flour to form a smooth, slightly sticky dough. Turn out onto a floured surface and knead until soft and satiny, not sticky, about 10 minutes. Place the dough in a clean bowl, cover tightly with plastic wrap, and set in a warm place to rise until doubled in bulk, about 1½ hours.

3. Meanwhile, sauté the bacon in a large skillet over medium-high heat until crisp, 7 to 8 minutes. Let cool in the skillet along with its rendered fat.

4. Preheat the oven to 425°F. Line two 15 × 10-inch baking sheets with parchment paper. Fill a pie plate or cake tin with water and place it on the bottom of the oven. (This will create steam while the bread bakes, and ensure a crispy crust.)

5. Punch down the dough, and then scrape the bacon along with all its fat into the center of the dough. With floured hands, knead until the bacon is evenly distributed throughout the dough.

6. Divide the dough in half and roll out each half on a floured surface to form an elongated oval, roughly 13 × 7 inches. Transfer each oval to a prepared baking sheet. Using a razor blade or a sharp knife, make 3 or 4 diagonal slashes from the center of the dough toward each side of the oval, as if drawing the veins on a leaf. Using your fingers, spread the slits apart to make wide gaps that will not close back up during the baking. Brush the *fougasses* all over with the beaten egg mixture; leave uncovered to rise for 20 minutes.

7. Bake the breads until crisp and golden brown, 25 to 30 minutes. Serve warm or at room temperature, and try to have a few friends around to share this bacon indulgence, so as not to be tempted to consume an entire *fougasse* yourself.

Makes 2 Large flatbreads

# creʃpeou

$C$*respeou* is the Provençal word for small pancakes or omelets. It also doubles as the name of a specific, splendid dish: Individual omelets are deliciously and alternately flavored with tomatoes, olives, artichokes, roasted peppers, and herbs and then layered to form a towering and colorful *gâteau,* which is then chilled, sliced into wedges, and served, accompanied by tomato sauce.

Look up the recipe for *crespeou* in a Provençal cookbook and you will be warned of *gros travail* (lots of work!), but savor it served as a first course at Nito Carpita's Mas de Cornud in St.-Remy after a day of cycling, and you'll no doubt be tempted to try the recipe. In addition to spectacular presentation and savor, a *crespeou* has other attributes: It can be made a couple of days in advance and it feeds a crowd.

My recipe is based on one Nito made the night my cycling group dined in one boisterous group, at a long table smack in the middle of the Mas de Cornud's kitchen. I have also taken to heart advice from local cookbooks that suggest flavoring the omelets *"à votre fantaisie."* Fantasies aside, I originally fretted over writing a recipe that calls unapologetically for 20 eggs, but then the very day I was constructing my *crespeou,* the *New York Times* ran an article stating that eggs may not be the bad cholesterol culprits that they have been portrayed as over the last three decades. Humpty Dumpty may get put back together again, and what better way than in a *crespeou de Provence*!

20 large eggs
Sea or coarse salt and freshly ground black pepper, to taste

OLIVE FILLING
1½ tablespoons olive oil
3 cloves garlic, minced
⅔ cup imported black or green olives, pitted and coarsely chopped
½ cup minced fresh parsley

ARTICHOKE FILLING
1½ tablespoons olive oil
1 small onion, minced
6 canned artichoke bottoms, drained and cut into ¼-inch dice
1 tablespoon minced fresh tarragon
2 teaspoons minced fresh thyme

TOMATO FILLING
1 tablespoon tomato paste
4 plum tomatoes, seeded and diced
⅓ cup shredded fresh basil

ROASTED PEPPER FILLING
2 roasted red or yellow bell peppers (page 135), diced
2 tablespoons minced fresh rosemary

Extra olive oil for making the omelets
Provençal Tomato Sauce (page 28), for serving

1. Clear an ample area of counter space for working, and line up 4 medium-size bowls. Break 5 eggs into each bowl, season with salt and pepper, and whisk each batch lightly with a fork until the yolks and whites are blended.

2. Make the olive filling: Heat the olive oil in a small skillet over medium heat. Add the garlic and sauté until softened and mellowed, 2 minutes. Stir in the olives and parsley and cook for 2 minutes more. Let cool a few minutes, and then combine with the first bowl of whisked eggs.

3. Make the artichoke filling: Heat the oil over medium heat in a small skillet. Add the onion and sauté until soft, 5 minutes. Add the artichokes, tarragon, and thyme and sauté for 2 minutes more. Let cool for a few minutes, and then mix into the second bowl of eggs.

4. Make the tomato filling: Simply whisk the tomato paste into the third bowl of eggs, and then gently fold in the diced tomatoes and the basil.

5. Make the roasted pepper filling: Fold the peppers and rosemary into the fourth bowl of eggs.

6. Preheat the oven to 375°F. Lightly oil a 9- to 9½-inch springform pan.

7. Make the omelets. Lightly coat a 9-inch nonstick omelet pan with olive oil and heat over medium heat. Half of each flavor of egg mixture will be used to make each omelet layer, so that there will be 8 layers in all. The flavors should be alternated, so proceed in whatever order strikes your fancy.

Pour half of one of the flavored egg mixtures into the hot pan. Cook without stirring until the omelet starts to bubble around the edges, 10 to 15 seconds. Then stir by pushing the cooked parts of the omelet toward the center with a rubber spatula and letting the uncooked parts run back outward towards the edges. Continue cooking in this manner until the bottom is set but the top is still

81

slightly wet and runny, 1½ to 2 minutes total cooking time. Gently slide the omelet, keeping it flat, with the less-cooked side up, into the springform pan. Repeat the process with half of another flavored egg mixture, adding more oil to the skillet if needed, and then layer on top of the first omelet. Continue in this manner until two of each flavored omelet has been made and layered alternately into the springform pan.

8. Bake the *crespeou* in the oven to set the runny parts of the omelets, about 20 minutes. Let cool to room temperature. Place a plate on top of the *crespeou* to weight it down slightly, and refrigerate for at least 2 hours or for as long as a day or two.

9. Serve the *crespeou* either chilled or at room temperature. Slice into thin wedges, and place on a plate with a thin pool of room-temperature Provençal Tomato Sauce.

MAKEƒ 16 to 20 ƒervingƒ

82

# trucHA

**t***rucha* is a Niçois specialty that looks like a close cousin of Italy's frittatas. However, the combination of flavors—garlic, golden raisins, Swiss chard, and pine nuts, distinguishes it as unabashedly Niçois. My recipe is based on the *trucha* served to me one full-moonlit evening at the popular Le Safari restaurant on the Cours Saleya in Vieux Nice. Finding this *trucha* most pleasing but a mite too filling as the first course of a Provençal dinner, I prefer to make mine ahead and offer small, room temperature wedges as an hors d'oeuvre with cocktails. This unusual omelet could also be served as the star of a luncheon or brunch.

2½ tablespoons golden raisins

¼ cup water

2 tablespoons pastis, such as Pernod or Ricard

1 pound Swiss chard, washed, stems and thick center
    ribs removed, leaves patted dry

2½ tablespoons olive oil

2 cloves garlic, minced

3 tablespoons pine nuts, lightly toasted

8 large eggs

Sea or coarse salt and freshly ground black pepper,
    to taste

3 tablespoons freshly grated Parmesan cheese

83

1. Preheat the broiler.

2. Combine the raisins, water, and *pastis* in a small saucepan; bring to a boil and simmer for 5 minutes. Remove from the heat, drain, and set aside.

3. Cut the Swiss chard leaves into ½-inch-wide strips. Heat the olive oil over medium heat in a 10- to 12-inch nonstick skillet. Add the garlic and sauté until softened and mellowed, 2 minutes. Add the chard and sauté until wilted, 3 to 4 minutes. Spread the chard evenly over the bottom of the skillet and sprinkle the raisins and pine nuts randomly over the top.

4. Beat the eggs until combined and foamy. Season with salt and pepper and pour into the skillet over the vegetable mixture. Cook over medium heat until the eggs begin to set around the edges.

Using a spatula, gently lift the cooked edges in order to let the uncooked egg run under the bottom. Continue cooking in this manner until the eggs are almost set on top.

5. Sprinkle the Parmesan over the top of the *trucha* and finish cooking it underneath the broiler, 3 to 4 inches from the heat, until set and light golden brown on top, 4 to 5 minutes. The *trucha* may be served at once or allowed to cool and served either warm or at room temperature. Cut into wedges or bite-size triangles.

*serves 4 as an omelet or 8 to 10 as an hors d'oeuvre*

# pan bagnat

**p**an bagnat, which translates literally as "bathed bread," has got to be one of the world's best sandwiches. A Niçois specialty sold in food shops and from street stands along the Côte d'Azur, this treat is made by splitting crusty French rolls in half and then filling them with a *salade niçoise* sort of mixture, whose delicious olive oil dressing then seeps into or "bathes" the bread. I've always found the sandwiches to be especially tasty when they've been stashed into a sack, and subjected to the bonus jiggle of a sunny morning's journey to some tranquil site. Here is how I like to make my *pan bagnat*.

> 2 cans (6½ ounces each) tuna, preferably oil-packed, drained
> 2 tablespoons capers, drained
> 1 bunch scallions, trimmed and minced
> ½ cup Niçois or Nyons olives, pitted and coarsely chopped
> 2 teaspoons grated lemon zest
> ¼ cup shredded fresh basil
> ⅓ cup fresh lemon juice
> 1½ tablespoons anchovy paste
> 2 cloves garlic, minced
> ½ cup fruity olive oil
> Sea or coarse salt and freshly ground black pepper, to taste
> 6 crusty white rolls, 4 to 5 inches in diameter
> Vine-ripened tomatoes, sliced
> Roasted red bell peppers (page 135), sliced
> Arugula leaves

85

1. Flake the tuna in a mixing bowl and toss with the capers, scallions, olives, lemon zest, and basil. In a smaller bowl, whisk together the lemon juice, anchovy paste, and garlic. Slowly whisk in the oil to make a vinaigrette. Season with salt and pepper and pour over the tuna mixture, tossing well.

2. Split the rolls in half horizontally. Divide the tuna salad between the 6 rolls, mounding onto the bottom half of each. Top with sliced tomatoes, sliced roasted red peppers, and a few arugula leaves. Sandwich the halves back together and let stand for at least 1 hour in order to let the dressing seep into the bread. Serve with plenty of napkins.

Makes 6 servings

## THE PEANUTS AND PLEASURES OF CHÂTEAU DES ALPILLES

Hôtel Château des Alpilles is a lovely nineteenth-century château, nestled at the end of a magnificent arcade of ancient trees on the outskirts of St.-Rémy. Happily, it is also home base when I and my fellow cyclists are pedaling about this spectacular area, with its rich history of Greeks, Romans, troubadours, prophets, poets, and painters.

In my opinion, one of the most rewarding days my groups spend cycling in Provence is the day we bike from the Château des Alpilles up to the perched city of Les Baux. Years ago, when I guided my first bicycle trips in this area, the policy was to transport our clients by van up the long hill to the entrance of Les Baux. Now we make the snaking, 6-kilometer climb through the moonlike landscape of Les Alpilles (little Alps) on bikes, and such an accomplishment always makes the visit to the often tourist-infested sights of Les Baux all the more memorable. It also makes what may sound like a rather ordinary bar nibble—a mix of peanuts and raisins—taste all the more splendid when savored after the fabulous descent back down the Baux hill, a

dip in the hotel's pool, and an icy beer, crisp glass of rosé, or potent *pastis* in the Château's elegant bar. There is something about the saltiness of the peanuts and the sweetness of the raisins that just hits the spot. At home, I make my version by mixing 1 can (12 ounces) salted cocktail peanuts, 1 cup lightly toasted whole almonds, ⅓ cup dark raisins, and ⅓ cup golden raisins. I serve this mix in small pottery bowls as an accompaniment to cocktails.

# ANCHOVY
# PASTRY FISH

W hen burning calories on a bicycle in France, it doesn't take much prompting to seize almost any moment as a guilt-less occasion for indulging in the local sips and savories. Some of the most memorable moments ensue when my groups gather after a full day's cycling for the traditional cocktail hour and ban-ter. Stories of the day's adventures are related and often exaggerated and idiosyncrasies endemic to our French hotel rooms inevitably compared. You'll know you're in Provence if all this good humor is enhanced by the passing of glasses of *pastis* and crisp mouth-fuls of salty anchovies wrapped in puff pastry.

I've always found the use of puff pastry in these quick-to-disappear nibbles a bit too rich for my taste and therefore prefer to make mine with a lemon-laced short-crust pastry. I also temper the intensity of the anchovies by blending creamy goat cheese into the filling. If you take the time to use a cookie cutter to cut the pastry into small fish shapes, the hors d'oeuvres will be all the more irresistible, and your guests will certainly think you've hooked the catch of the day.

87

PASTRY

1¼ cups unbleached all-purpose flour

1 tablespoon finely grated lemon zest

8 tablespoons (1 stick) chilled unsalted butter, cut
    into small pieces

2 teaspoons imported Dijon mustard

2 to 3 tablespoons ice water

ANCHOVY FILLING

1 can (2 ounces) flat anchovy fillets, drained

3 cloves garlic

½ cup parsley leaves

3 ounces soft white goat cheese, at room temperature

1 tablespoon fruity olive oil

1 large egg beaten with 1 tablespoon water

88

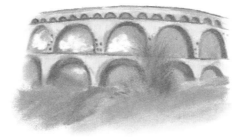

1. Make the pastry: Place the flour, lemon zest, and butter in a
food processor and pulse until the mixture resembles coarse meal.
Add the mustard and enough water so that the dough begins to
form a ball while you pulse the machine on and off. Shape the pastry
into a disk, wrap in plastic, and refrigerate for at least 30 minutes.

2. Make the filling: Place the anchovies, garlic, and parsley
together on a cutting board; mince all together to form a pastelike

blend. Using a fork, mash the goat cheese in a small bowl. Add the anchovy mixture and continue mashing until well blended. Add the olive oil and mash it into the filling as well.

3. Preheat the oven to 450°F. Line two 15 × 12-inch baking sheets with parchment paper.

4. On a lightly floured surface, roll out the chilled pastry dough ¼ inch thick. Using a 1½- to 2-inch fish-shaped cookie cutter or other similarly sized shape of choice, cut out an even number of shapes, gathering up and rerolling the scraps. Place scant ½ teaspoons of the filling in the centers of half of the cut-out shapes. Moisten the edges of the dough with a little water, and top each with one of the remaining shapes. Pinch together with your fingers to securely seal in the filling and arrange the pastries ½ inch apart on the prepared baking sheets. Brush the pastries lightly all over with the beaten egg mixture.

5. Bake the pastries until puffed and golden brown, about 10 minutes. Serve hot, warm, or at room temperature, within a couple hours of baking for the best taste.

Makes about 48 pastries

89

# ARRIVING IN
# NICE

Nice's welcoming name must be more than a coincidence, for Nice is just about the nicest port of arrival in all of Europe. For starters, it can be reached by a convenient, direct, and usually half-empty flight from New York, which has become the favorite mode of transport for feeding my ever-growing Provençal passions. The approach to Nice from the air is simply spectacular, with tantalizing views of the expansive sapphire-blue Mediterranean sea and glimpses of the glitzy grandeur of the Côte d'Azur before a swoop down across Nice's curved Baie d'Anges, and a landing at the city's friendly little airport. Renting a car is a cinch, as is the short seaside drive into the heart of Nice. Once in the city, I like to book a hotel room with a view as splendid as the ones that inspired Matisse's paintings in this vibrant-hued paradise. The flowery and terraced Hôtel la Perouse, with its rambling charm and views of Nice's pebbled beach and famous palm-lined Promenade des Anglais, more than suits my needs.

I then always walk directly to Vieux Nice, or Old Nice, to immerse myself in the colorful and fragrant daily flower and food market on the Cours Saleya. I like to approach the market via rue St.-François-de-Paule, because three of my favorite shops are located on this short street. First, there is the quaint, well-known olive and olive oil shop Alziari, selling Niçois olives, of course, along with golden olive oil packed in collectible yellow and blue tins, olive-wood utensils, soaps, and herbs.

Just a hop up the street is Aver, an inviting 170-year-old sweet shop whose windows are filled with fabulous still lifes of Nice's *fruits confits.* The shop also sells fine chocolates and pastries. Next door is Le Moulin des Caracoles, filled with an irresistible array of Provence's best regional products: fabric, wine, olives, honey, books, and perfume.

Next thing I know, I'm blissfully in the midst of the bustling Cours Saleya, marveling over the exquisite displays of gorgeous green asparagus, violet-tipped artichokes, sun-drenched tomatoes, plump red strawberries, and woodsy mushrooms, depending on the time of year. The toughest decision of my day centers on whether to cull an assortment of picnic goods from the market for lunch and people-watching on the beach or to succumb to

the temptations of one of the many outdoor restaurants that spill into the cours. If the former wins out, then I'll head to Charcuterie Julien, on the corner of rue de la Poissonnerie, just off the cours, to pick up the perfect Niçois picnic fare—*pan bagnat*—along with a slice or two of the shop's wonderful pizza, topped lusciously with eggplant, tomatoes, zucchini, olives, anchovies, or onions. En route to the beach, I'll be sure to pause briefly in front of the cheerful yellow neoclassical house at the far end of the Cours Saleya, for it was here that Matisse painted for seventeen years of his time in Nice, in the fourth-floor *atelier*.

If I decide not to picnic, then my lunch spot will be one of two favorite market-area restaurants, Le Safari and La Merenda. Le Safari has great grilled fish and a top-notch version of the unique Niçois Swiss chard omelet known as *trucha*. La Merenda is a tiny restaurant with fire-engine-red tablecloths topped with crocks of colorful tea roses. It is known for its authentic old-fashioned Niçois specialties, and few can resist its super-rich and creamy fresh pasta tossed with emerald-green *pistou*.

Museums beckon for post-prandial diversion and enrichment. I'm always game for the boost in spirits that comes from looking at happy canvases and cutouts at the Musée Matisse up in the Cimiez section of Nice, now that it has at last reopened after several years of renovations. While it was closed, I often found myself enjoying an afternoon at the Musée National Marc Chagall or taking a leisurely drive out of Nice to visit Escoffier's birthplace and culinary museum in Villenueve-Loubet or the splendid Musée Picasso in Antibes, housed in a former Grimaldi family seaside estate.

Evenings in Nice are best devoted to moonlit strolls along the Promenade des Anglais, with lots of stops to peek into the grand hotels that line it. Dinner back in Vieux Nice is hard to resist, though the *bouillabaisse* at Bistrot Michel, not far from the palatial Hôtel Negresco can be mighty tempting, too. Sleep comes readily back at Hôtel la Perouse, with the sound of distant lapping waves singing their Mediterranean lullaby.

# MEDITERRANEAN
# MARVELS

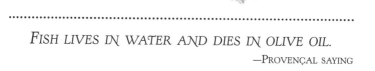

> *FISH LIVES IN WATER AND DIES IN OLIVE OIL.*
> —PROVENÇAL SAYING

the bicycling trips I guide in Provence are anchored inland, in some of the most serene and blessed olive oil-producing microclimates. These trips do not descend to the renowned sea-side resorts of the Côte d'Azur, where any fish lover must go to sample the freshest and most inspired creations of the Mediter-ranean. So, when not pedaling my way about the agricultural riches of the Vaucluse, I head for the pleasure-loving ports of the Riviera, where fashion, fish, and olive oil fuse wondrously.

A ferry crossing to Porquerolles, a car-forsaken island off the coast of Hyères, promises continued transport on two wheels along with splendid dining on *la simplicité et la fraîcheur des produits de la mer* ("the simple freshness of locally caught seafood") at the lovely, laid-back L'Auberge des Glycines. If I'm not slipping my spoon into a silky bowl of *bourride* laden with island fish, then I'm probably lost in a mound of mussels poached in Porquerolles wine, or a platter of rock shrimp fric-asseed in olive oil, or a plate of red mullets stuffed with glis-tening tapenade.

Cassis is another sunny stomping ground favored for its

zigzagging *calanques* and the great calamari, cod, and monkfish dished forth in the bustling old fishing port's quayside restaurants. I can readily bypass Brigette Bardot's St.-Tropez and film festival-crazed Cannes for the worn seawalls of Antibes. Echoes of F. Scott Fitzgerald's "deferential palms cooling flushed facades" of "rose-colored hotels" linger and mingle with honeyed scents of pittosporum and the creeping appetite for something fishy, consumed while tucked into a corner of a little restaurant in Vieux Antibes.

A visit to Eze, north along the Côte d'Azur *corniche* roads, is truly like hooking the best catch of the day, for Eze is considered the most steeply perched of all the *villages perchés* in Provence, and a car makes a fine mode of ascent, as far as I'm concerned. It is said that German philosopher Friedrich Nietzsche once walked all the way up to Eze from the seashore below, a trek that supposedly made his head spin and inspired the third portion of *Thus Spake Zarathustra*. Obviously, Nietzsche never lunched at the top, as I did, on grilled fish *à la vierge*, a *vierge* with a view, I might add!

# cAbiLLAud deſ boɾieſ

cᴀʙɪʟʟᴀᴜᴅ, or cod, both fresh and dried (*morue*), is beloved in Provence and is one of the few Riviera fish to appear regularly on inland restaurant menus. This unique recipe, in which milky white cod fillets are crisped with bread crumbs spiced with assorted peppercorns, ginger, nutmeg, cinnamon, and curry powder is the specialty of chef Michel Ducellier at Les Bories—a luxurious hotel/restaurant in Gordes with rooms that look across peaceful acres of orchards and olive groves. Les Bories is named after Provence's historic beehive-shaped, dry stone huts, believed to have been used in past centuries either as villagers' refuges from the plague or as shelters for shepherds. Restaurant guests are fortunate enough to dine by candlelight under the cozy, white stone dome of the restaurant's restored *borie*.

*Onion Confit*
¼ cup olive oil
3 large onions, sliced into thin rings
2 to 3 cups Gigondas wine, or other rich, red
    Rhône-style wine
¼ cup balsamic or red wine vinegar
3 tablespoons honey
Sea or coarse salt and freshly ground black
    pepper, to taste

*Cod*
1½ cups fresh French bread crumbs
1½ teaspoons coarsely cracked mixed peppercorns
    (white, green, pink, and black)
1 teaspoon ground ginger
1 teaspoon ground cinnamon
1 teaspoon curry powder
½ teaspoon ground nutmeg
Pinch of cayenne pepper
Sea or coarse salt, to taste
5 tablespoons olive oil
3 pounds fresh cod fillets, divided into 6 portions

1. To make the onion confit, heat the olive oil in a large, deep skillet over medium-high heat. Add the onions and sauté until quite soft, about 15 minutes. Pour in 2 cups of the wine, the vinegar, and honey; simmer the mixture, uncovered, stirring occasionally, until thick and jamlike in consistency, about 45 minutes. If the mixture seems to be drying up too much, add more wine. Season the confit with salt and pepper, and keep warm over low heat. The confit will keep for up to 3 days. Reheat over low heat in a saucepan.

97.

2. When ready to cook the cod, preheat the oven to 425°F.

3. Combine the bread crumbs with the cracked pepper, ginger, cinnamon, curry, nutmeg, and cayenne in a small bowl. Season with salt and moisten by drizzling with 3 tablespoons of the olive oil. Brush a baking pan large enough to hold the cod fillets in a single layer with another tablespoon olive oil. Arrange the fillets in the pan and press a light layer of seasoned bread crumbs evenly over the top of each fillet. Drizzle with the remaining tablespoon olive oil.

4. Bake the cod until the crumbs are golden and the fish is just cooked through the center, 15 to 20 minutes. Serve the fillets at once atop a bed of the warmed onion confit.

makes 6 servings

## SOME ENCHANTED CYCLING

*I*t was a particularly challenging day of Provençal cycling that physically introduced my tour group to the true meaning of *village perché,* or hilltop village. The day's itinerary had included sightseeing stops at many of these most beautiful, honey-colored sites in the "hide and chic" Petit Lubéron: Roussillon, famed for its red ocher cliffs; Lacoste, dominated by the eerie ruins of the Marquis de Sade's château; and Ménerbes, whose shiplike silhouette is now overshadowed by the lingering celebrity of its one-time resident, the writer Peter Mayle. Then down and back up, up, up to the restful tranquility of our Gordes hotel. The aches that wouldn't be soothed by dips in Les Bories's indoor pool or soaks in hot baths, were spiritually cured with a twilight excursion to the solitary twelfth-century Cistercian Abbaye de Sénanque to hear the monks chant their 6 o'clock vespers.

While I wouldn't mind having my own private *borie* as the perfect backdrop to enhance Les Bories's cod (see page 96), I have instead managed to content myself with serving the fish on a confit of Gigondas-simmered onions, a recipe suggestion from the wine cooperative in the village of Gigondas.

# sausage-scaled cod fillets

∽

to my knowledge, the practice of creatively restoring the look of scales to cooked fish began with setting cucumber crescents into aspic on cold, whole poached salmon. Next came scaling fish fillets with paper thin slices of potato that turned irresistibly crispy as the fillets were sautéed. But leave it to a Provençal chef with a weak spot for his mother's and grandmother's cooking, and the charge of a top restaurant in Paris, to invent the tastiest and prettiest scales of all! Indeed, Christian Constant's longing for the herb-scented hills and salty shores of Provence shines through in every brilliant bite of the spicy chorizo-scaled cod he serves at Les Ambassadeurs at the Hôtel de Crillon, in Paris.

99

The recipe is simple to prepare, and its sublimity comes from using the freshest cod and best-spiced regional *saucisson sec.* In Provence, the famous *saucisson d'Arles,* scented with black peppercorns, paprika, and garlic is a fine choice. Stateside I've had good luck with sliced pepperoni, Genoa salami, or Abruzze sausage purchased in Italian markets. Surround the fillets with Roasted Ratatouille (see Index) for a spectacular feast.

*4 skinned fresh cod fillets, about 6 ounces each*
*Sea salt and freshly ground black pepper, to taste*
*1 large egg yolk beaten with 1 tablespoon water*
*4 ounces semihard sausage, such as Genoa salami, Abruzze*
*    sausage, or pepperoni, sliced paper-thin*
*2 tablespoons olive oil*

1. Season the fish generously with salt and pepper. Using a pastry brush, brush the tops of each fillet liberally with the egg mixture. Press the sausage slices on each fillet in overlapping rows to cover the top completely and create a scalelike pattern.

2. Heat the olive oil in a large skillet over medium-high heat. Sauté the fillets, sausage side down, until crisped and lightly brown, 3 to 4 minutes. Carefully, flip the fillets over and continue sautéing until the fish is just barely cooked through the center, another 3 to 4 minutes. Serve at once.

Makes 4 servings

# WHole grilled fiSH
# À La vierge

Sea bass grilled over an aromatic bed of dried fennel stalks is the quintessential Provençal fish dish. But dried fennel stalks are seemingly nonexistent in North America, so I was delighted to discover this equally delicious whole grilled fish recipe in a little restaurant in the picturesque perched village of Eze along the Côte d'Azur. While *daurade,* a coveted Mediterranean fish with firm white flesh, was the fish grilled in this instance, what really tickled my fancy was the virgin olive oil sauce with its whole cloves of roasted garlic, rosy bits of ripe tomato, and abundance of slivered green basil leaves. Such is the sublimity of *à la vierge* in the recipe's title.

Good whole fish choices for grilling in North America include small red snapper, sea bass, pompano, or even trout.

OLIVE OIL SAUCE
*15 cloves garlic, unpeeled*
*2 medium vine-ripened tomatoes*
*1½ cups extra-virgin olive oil*
*½ cup slivered fresh basil*
*Sea or coarse salt and freshly ground black pepper, to taste*

101

FISH
*4 whole fish (see above; about 1½ pounds each), scaled and gutted*
*Sea or coarse salt and freshly ground black pepper, to taste*
*Several sprigs of fresh rosemary*
*Olive oil, for grilling*

1. Preheat the oven to 350°F.

2. To make the olive oil sauce, wrap the garlic cloves in aluminum foil and roast on a baking sheet in the oven until softened but not so mushy they begin to disintegrate, about 25 minutes. Open the foil and allow the garlic to cool. When cool enough to handle, squeeze the cloves from the skins and place in a small saucepan.

3. Bring a large pot of salted water to a boil, then plunge in the tomatoes for exactly 1 minute. Drain and slip off and discard the

skins. Seed the tomatoes, cut into small dice, and add to the garlic in the saucepan.

4. Pour in the olive oil, stir in the basil, and season to taste with salt and pepper. The sauce may be prepared ahead and allowed to stand at room temperature for up to 6 hours before warming and serving.

5. Prepare charcoal for grilling.

6. Season the cavities of the fish with salt and pepper and add a few springs of rosemary. Brush the outsides of the fish lightly with olive oil. When the fire is ready, grill the fish on an oiled rack, 5 to 6 inches from the heat. Grill the fish until lightly charred on the underside, 7 to 8 minutes. Flip the fish over and continue grilling until the flesh is just cooked through the center, another 7 to 8 minutes. While the fish is grilling, heat the sauce over low heat until warmed through. Serve the fish whole, on large dinner plates, accompanied by a bowl of the warm olive oil sauce for spooning over the fish.

102

Makes 4 servings

# gigot de Mer

The title of this recipe literally translates as "leg of lamb of the sea." It is so named because a thick piece of fish is studded with garlic in the same way that a leg of lamb is prepared for roasting. Because the fish is then placed in a stew pot and surrounded by a ratatouille-like vegetable mélange—which helps to keep the fish delightfully moist as it bakes—the dish also goes by the name of *daube de poisson*.

Whatever the title, this is a wonderful way to cook sword-fish or tuna when the weather is too inclement for outdoor grilling. The fish is served sliced atop all the vegetables from the stew, making for a terrific one-pot meal, especially when accompanied by crusty bread for sopping up the delicious juices. I personally think of *gigot de mer* as an unusual way of making a hearty winter meal of fish, though in Provence it is often served cold for a summer luncheon or dinner. A light red Côtes du Rhône wine is the perfect pour.

2 medium eggplants
2 tablespoons sea or coarse salt
2 pieces center-cut swordfish or
　　2 tuna steaks (2 pounds each),
　　about 2 inches thick
4 large cloves garlic, slivered
6 anchovy fillets, drained
2 teaspoons grated lemon zest
¼ cup olive oil
2 large onions, sliced thinly
3 medium zucchini, trimmed and cut into ¾-inch dice
1 red bell pepper, stemmed, seeded, and cut into ¾-inch squares
1 yellow bell pepper, stemmed, seeded, and cut into ¾-inch squares
1 tablespoon herbes de Provence
1 can (28 ounces) diced tomatoes
1¼ cups dry red wine
2 tablespoons drained capers

103

1. Peel the eggplant in stripes, leaving alternating strips of skin in place. Cut into 1-inch cubes, toss with the salt, and let stand

in a colander placed in a bowl to drain for 30 minutes.

2. Meanwhile, make several ½-inch-deep slits with the point of a sharp knife on both sides of the fish steaks. Insert the garlic slivers into the cuts and let stand at room temperature while preparing the rest of the ingredients.

3. Mince the anchovies and lemon zest together to form a paste. Set aside in a small bowl.

4. Preheat the oven to 350°F.

5. Heat the oil in a large Dutch oven over medium-high heat. Add the onions and sauté until very soft, about 15 minutes. Using your hands, wring as much water as you can from the salted eggplant. Add the eggplant to the pot along with the zucchini and peppers. Season with the *herbes de Provence* and continue sautéing, stirring frequently, for 15 minutes more.

6. Add the tomatoes, wine, the reserved anchovy-lemon mixture, and capers to the pot. Stir well and cook for 5 minutes. Immerse the fish steaks into the vegetables, spooning about half of the vegetables over the top of the fish. Cover the pot and transfer to the center of the oven. Bake undisturbed until the fish is cooked through the center, 45 minutes to 1 hour.

7. Let the stew stand for 10 minutes and then carefully transfer the fish to a cutting board. Slice the fish ½ inch thick and serve atop plenty of vegetables from the stew pot.

Makes 6 to 8 servings

# Sautéed Skate Wings with Lemon and Capers

∾

**t**he accordionlike appearance and silky texture of skate wings often make me think that "angel wings" might be a more apt name. In Provence skate, or *raie* as the French call it, may be served napped with a rich tomato sauce, or poached and placed atop a bed of slivered and simmered fennel, or sautéed in the simple and classic manner presented here—with fish-friendly lemon and capers.

As other species of fish perceived to be more upscale have become increasingly scarce in North American waters, skate has begun to appear more frequently in fish markets and on restaurant menus. Skate's availability combined with its reasonable price and the bonus of an easy and delicious recipe should hopefully encourage "afishionados" to make this staple Provençal fish a frequent, winged fryer on home turf.

¾ cup instant-blend flour, such as Wondra
Sea or coarse salt and freshly ground pepper,
     to taste
4 skate wings (about 8 ounces each), boned
2 tablespoons olive oil
4 to 5 tablespoons unsalted butter
½ cup dry white wine
3 tablespoons fresh lemon juice
1 lemon, peeled, seeded, and thinly sliced
2 tablespoons drained capers
¼ cup minced fresh parsley

1. Season the flour with salt and pepper and spread in a shallow dish such as a pie plate. Dredge the skate wings in the flour, turning to coat evenly on both sides.

2. Heat the olive oil with 2 tablespoons of the butter in a large skillet over medium-high heat. Sauté the skate wings, in batches if necessary, until lightly browned and crisped on the outside and just cooked through, 3 to 4 minutes per side. Transfer the cooked skate to a platter and keep warm.

3. Add the wine to the skillet and deglaze over high heat. When all but 2 tablespoons of the wine has evaporated, 3 to 5 minutes, reduce the heat to low, and add 2 tablespoons more butter, the lemon juice, lemon slices, and capers. Once the butter has melted, taste the sauce and if it seems too tart, swirl in the remaining 1 tablespoon butter. Stir in the parsley. Pour the sauce over the skate wings and serve at once.

Makes 4 servings

# Quayside Calamari Salad

After a long morning of lazing in the sun along the *calanques* of Cassis, a body can crave an umbrella-shaded luncheon table at any of the many good fish restaurants that fringe the quays of the town's bustling old port. A beaded ice bucket with a bottle of the local Cassis white wine should assuage the parched palate, while plates of cool calamari salad glistening with olive oil and matchstick strips of red and yellow pepper can work magic on salt-air-induced hunger pangs.

Peeling the peppers in the recipe before cooking makes them extra tender, and the task is easily accomplished with a sharp, swivel-bladed vegetable peeler.

¾ cup dry white wine
¾ cup water
2 pounds cleaned squid, tentacles left whole and
    bodies cut into ¾-inch rings
2 ribs celery, sliced diagonally ½ inch thick
⅓ cup fruity olive oil
2 shallots, minced
3 cloves garlic, minced
Pinch of hot red pepper flakes
3 tablespoons fresh lemon juice
1½ tablespoons pastis, such as Pernod or Ricard
½ red bell pepper, stemmed, seeded, peeled, and cut into very
    thin matchstick strips 1½ inches long
1 yellow bell pepper, stemmed, seeded, peeled, and cut into
    very thin matchstick strips 1½ inches long
¼ cup minced fresh parsley
¼ cup slivered fresh basil
Sea or coarse salt and freshly ground black pepper, to taste
Soft lettuce leaves, for serving

1. Combine the wine and water in a deep skillet and bring to a simmer over medium-high heat. Add the squid rings and poach until they just begin to lose their translucency and are tender, 2½ to 3 minutes. Remove from the skillet with a slotted spoon, draining well, and combine with the celery in a large mixing bowl. Add the squid tentacles to the simmering liquid and poach until tender, 3 to 3½ minutes. Remove with a slotted spoon, draining well, and add to the mixing bowl. Boil the poaching

liquid over high heat until it is reduced by half, 10 to 15 minutes.

2. Meanwhile, heat the olive oil in a medium-size skillet over medium heat. Add the shallots, garlic, and red pepper flakes and sauté until softened, 5 minutes. Add the reduced poaching liquid, lemon juice, *pastis,* and peppers; simmer to blend the flavors and just barely cook the peppers, 5 minutes more. Pour the hot dressing over the squid and toss thoroughly to coat. Let cool to room temperature, stirring occasionally. Add the parsley and basil and toss again. Season the salad with salt and pepper.

Transfer to a serving bowl and refrigerate for at least 3 hours before serving. Serve chilled, mounded onto lettuce-lined plates.

Makes 4 to 6 servings

# Spicy Squid and Chick-pea Ragoût

the rule of thumb for achieving tender-tasting squid is to either sauté it very quickly or simmer it for a long period of time. The latter technique governs this deeply flavored seafood stew based on recipes with octopus that I have savored in many a Riviera restaurant. Since I have been continually disappointed by octopus I have eaten in the United States and am the sort of person who can enthusiastically dine on squid, or calamari, seven nights a week, opting for squid in this ragoût was a natural choice.

Chick-peas are the beloved legume of Provence and are most frequently prepared there as a simple salad drizzled with olive oil. I decided to add them to my recipe to lend extra body to this characteristically saucy ragoût, as well as delightful contrast to the texture of the squid. When I first tested the recipe, it sent a couple of my Italian dinner guests into absolute ecstasy; this has given me the confidence to suggest serving the squid in an acceptable Niçois style over a bed of soft and creamy Italian polenta.

3 tablespoons olive oil
3 ounces slab bacon, cut into ¼-inch dice
1 large onion, minced
3 carrots, peeled and minced
3 ribs celery, minced
5 cloves garlic, minced
2 teaspoons fennel seeds
1 teaspoon saffron threads
1 to 2 teaspoons hot red pepper flakes
3½ pounds cleaned squid, tentacles left whole
    and bodies cut into 1-inch rings
⅓ cup brandy
1 cup dry red wine
1 can (28 ounces) tomatoes, diced
2 tablespoons tomato paste
2 tablespoons grated orange zest
Sea or coarse salt and freshly ground black pepper, to taste
1 can (15 ounces) chick-peas, drained
½ cup slivered fresh basil

1. Heat the oil over medium heat in a large Dutch oven. Add the bacon and cook until browned, about 5 minutes. Add the onion, carrots, celery, garlic, fennel seeds, saffron, and hot red pepper flakes. Sauté until the vegetables are softened, 7 to 10 minutes.

2. Add the squid rings and tentacles to the pot, toss with the vegetables, and cook just until the squid begins to lose its translucency, 3 to 4 minutes. Remove the Dutch oven from the heat. Pour in the brandy, and standing back, carefully light it with a long kitchen match. When the flames die out, pour in the red wine, return the pot to medium heat, and continue cooking for 2 minutes. There should be quite a bit of liquid in the pot at this point.

3. Remove the Dutch oven from the heat and set aside temporarily. Using a ladle and tilting the pot, remove as much of the liquid from the ragoût as possible and transfer to another saucepan. Bring the liquid in the saucepan to a boil and let it cook until reduced by half, 15 to 20 minutes. Pour the reduced liquid back over the squid and return the ragoût to the stove on medium-low heat.

4. Add the diced tomatoes, tomato paste, and orange zest to the ragoût, stirring well. Season with salt and pepper. Cover the pot and let the ragoût simmer, stirring occasionally, until the squid is very tender, 1½ hours.

5. Add the chick-peas to the ragoût and continue simmering for another 15 to 20 minutes. Serve the squid ragoût in flat, wide bowls, garnished with some slivered basil.

Makes 8 to 10 servings

## ESCAPING TO CASSIS

Cassis, a quaint town unrelated to the syrupy black-currant liqueur of the same name, is one of my favorite ports on the French Riviera. Due east of swarthy Marseilles, Cassis seems miles away, with its colorful old fishing harbor chockful of lively quay-side restaurants and its stunningly unique *calanques*—long narrow inlets where sparkling emerald Mediterranean waters zigzag between a jutting series of jagged limestone cliffs. So magical is this relatively undeveloped Riviera idyll that I often find myself taking seriously the town's tongue-in-cheek motto: "If you've seen Paris and not Cassis, you've seen nothing."

Whenever feasible, I love to pass a perfectly lazy Provençal day sunning and swimming for extended morning hours along the *calanques*. Now, bicycling up and down the mountain ranges of inland Provence may work up a sweat, but there's nothing like seaside languor for bringing on a ravenous thirst and appetite. Grilled fish and briny calamari salads are always especially tasty after sunning in Cassis, but it is the local white wine that always lingers longest in memory. My favorite American wine writer and importer, Kermit Lynch, summed it all up in *Adventures on the Wine Route:*

> Cassis [white wine] has a brilliant sun-drenched color and it marries perfectly with the local cuisine. This is garlic-and-olive-oil land, and in the local restaurants it would be crazy to drink a Muscadet or Montrachet with the catch of the day. . . . But then of course Cassis tastes better at Cassis! Debussy sounds better after a walk through the foggy, puddled streets of late-night Paris. You are in the midst of the atmosphere that created it. The wine is not different, the music is not different. You are.

# Seared Scallops with Candied Tomatoes and Basil

My culinary antennae perk up any time I spy scallops on a restaurant menu in Provence because I'm always looking for new ideas to bring home and try using Nantucket's prized bay scallops. This recipe hits the jackpot. Sea scallops, available year-round, are the type used in Provence, but I happily discovered that Nantucket's bay scallops, harvested only between November and March, could be used for a local spin. The oven-drying of the tomatoes deepens or "candies" the flavor so much that even winter tomatoes become intense enough to mimic the recipe's original, sun-drenched inspiration. How restorative it is to have warmth of palate when warmth of place is only a memory.

18 small ripe plum tomatoes
6 tablespoons fruity olive oil
2 cloves garlic, minced
2 teaspoons sugar
1 tablespoon herbes de Provence
1 tablespoon balsamic or red wine vinegar
Sea or coarse salt and freshly ground black pepper, to taste
1½ pounds fresh bay scallops
½ cup slivered fresh basil

1. Preheat the oven to 375°F.

2. Bring a large pot of salted water to a boil and then plunge in the tomatoes for exactly 1 minute. Drain and slip off and discard the skins. Cut the tomatoes in half lengthwise and remove the seeds. Arrange the tomatoes, cut side up, in a 13 × 9-inch baking dish. Drizzle with 3 tablespoons of the olive oil, and sprinkle with the garlic, sugar, *herbes de Provence,* and vinegar. Season with salt and pepper. Bake until shriveled and randomly caramelized with crusty brown patches, 40 to 45 minutes. Reduce the heat to 250°F to keep warm while searing the scallops.

3. Heat the remaining 3 tablespoons oil in a large skillet over medium-high heat. Pat the scallops dry with paper towels and sear them in the hot oil, shaking the pan until the scallops are barely cooked through, 2½ to 3 minutes total cooking time. Sprinkle with the basil and remove from heat.

4. On each plate, make a bed of 6 candied tomato halves. Spoon the scallops over the top and serve at once.

Makes 6 servings

# grilled seafood brochettes

Colorful mixtures of fish and shellfish skewered with herbs and citrus are served at many waterfront restaurants along the entire Côte d'Azur. I love ordering one variation or another for late lunches after lazy days of sunning, but these brochettes could also make a cooling and light dinner offering on a sultry summer night. Lacing many bay leaves between the bacon-wrapped scallops and the unshelled shrimp gives these beautiful brochettes a heavy dose of Mediterranean flair and flavor. They may be served as is, hot and charred from the grill, or further embellished by the same luscious olive oil sauce that is spooned over the Whole Grilled Fish à la Vierge (see Index).

> 1 pound sea scallops, or 1 pound boned and skinned
>     monkfish, cut into 1-inch cubes (you need
>     24 scallops or cubes)
> 1 pound large (16- to 18-count) shrimp,
>     in their shells
> 3 tablespoons fruity olive oil
> 3 tablespoons fresh lemon juice
> Sea or coarse salt and freshly ground
>     black pepper, to taste
> 24 whole bay leaves
> 8 slices bacon
> 4 thick slices lemon, halved

1. Prepare charcoal for grilling.

2. Combine the scallops or monkfish with the shrimp in a medium-size bowl. Drizzle with the olive oil and the lemon juice, tossing to coat evenly. Season the fish with salt and pepper and let stand 30 minutes.

3. Meanwhile, put the bay leaves in a small bowl and cover with boiling water to soften them. Let stand 10 minutes, then drain.

4. To assemble the brochettes, have ready 4 long metal skewers. Cut each slice of bacon crosswise into thirds. Wrap a third of a slice around each scallop or piece of monkfish so that the ends overlap on one side. Use the skewer to secure the ends of the bacon by taking care to make sure the skewer point pierces the overlapping

portion of the bacon when threading. Assemble each skewer in this order: bacon-wrapped scallop (or monkfish), bay leaf, bacon-wrapped scallop, shrimp pierced in a C-shape through both the top and the tail, lemon slice, shrimp, and then back to the scallop/bay leaf sequence. Two more shrimp and another lemon slice should be added before ending the skewer with two final scallops and bay leaves. In the end, each skewer should contain 6 bacon-wrapped scallops, 6 bay leaves, 4 shrimp, and 2 lemon slice halves.

5. Grill the brochettes over hot coals, 4 to 5 inches from the heat. Baste with any remaining olive oil and lemon juice marinade. Turn the skewers frequently to cook all sides and crisp the bacon. The brochettes should take 7 to 9 minutes total cooking time. Serve at once.

Makes 4 servings

# crevettes carpentras

Cyclists who come to pedal Provence in April and May will see the land at its greenest, with fireworkslike bursts of color splashing forth from bright yellow sprays of Scotch broom, fields of vermilion poppies, and clusters of the same deep purple irises that had once inspired Van Gogh. In markets and roadside stands there will be signs advertising *fraises* (strawberries) *de Carpentras*. My cyclists will certainly sample these wonderful strawberries, but most will never visit Carpentras, a large Vaucluse town of 30,000, also known for its winter truffle market and spectacularly decorated synagogue, because a formidable maze of highly trafficked motorways crisscrosses the outskirts of the main city.

I frequently base myself in Carpentras for a night or two while doing research work on routes and activities before a trip I'm leading begins. Carpentras, with its bookshops and one-hour photo kiosks, is a good place to get errands accomplished and an amiable town for grabbing an unpretentious but satisfying meal. I particularly like Restaurant le Marigo, in the central and civilized pedestrian zone. The restaurant has crisp white walls, timbered apricot-hued ceilings, and only a dozen small tables. Too many or too few glasses of Le Marigo's special, 10-franc, wine-of-the-month can make the iridescent violet staircase leading up to the kitchen aesthetically unbearable, but if you've ordered the terrific *crevettes,* or shrimp, bathed in garlic and *pastis,* you should be too busy peeling the shells, savoring the pink meat, and mopping up the delicious sauce with every slice of *baguette* in your basket to notice.

⅔ cup fruity olive oil
¼ cup pastis, such as Pernod or Ricard
6 cloves garlic, coarsely chopped
2 teaspoons fennel seeds
½ cup minced fresh parsley
3 pounds medium shrimp (21- to 25-count), in their shells
Sea or coarse salt and freshly ground black pepper, to taste
1 whole lemon, cut in half lengthwise, halves thinly sliced

1. Preheat the oven to 425°F.

2. Whisk together the olive oil, *pastis,* garlic, fennel seeds, and parsley. Pour over the shrimp in a medium-size bowl, tossing to coat the shrimp thoroughly. Season with salt and pepper. Transfer the

shrimp to a gratin dish just large enough to hold them in a single layer. Tuck the lemon slices among the shrimp.

3. Bake the shrimp, turning them once halfway through the cooking time, until tender and just cooked through, 15 to 20 minutes. Serve the shrimp piping hot from the gratin dish in a communal fashion, or portion out into individual shallow dishes. Be sure to provide an extra dish for the discarded shells, lots of French bread for dunking into the sauce, and plenty of napkins for wiping happy but messy hands.

Makes 6 servings

117

# Moules Les Domaines

Whether at home or abroad, on a bike, in a car, or on foot, I brake for mussels. This recipe combines the best of all worlds because it was discovered after I bid farewell to one of my cycling groups at the train station in the grand walled city of Avignon. Left with time for a leisurely stroll through its bustling streets and squares, and soothed by a visit to the Simone Martini frescoes in the Petit Palace, I found myself, come noontime, seated in Les Domaines Wine Bar on the colorful place de l'Horloge. Lured by the prospect of tasting some interesting regional wines, I naturally ordered the *moules gratinées,* and soon a deli-

cious dozen mussels arrived sizzling with a crusty topping of bread crumbs, ground hazelnuts, minced garlic, and parsley, under-scored by a hint of *pastis*. Not only did the flavors pair perfect-ly with the delectable, subtle spiciness of the white Crozes-Hermitage in my wineglass, but I knew the recipe would be a good traveler.

Serve the mussels as a light luncheon dish with a salad or as a first course at a more elaborate dinner. They may also be passed as an hors d'oeuvre if guests are comfortable with inhaling them directly from the half-shell like raw oysters. Don't forget to seize the opportunity to pour one of the rich white wines from the Rhône or even one of the knock-off California "Rhône Ranger" Viogniers.

*1½ cups dried bread crumbs*
*½ cup toasted skinned hazelnuts*
*3 cloves garlic, minced*
*½ cup minced fresh parsley*
*⅓ cup olive oil*
*2 tablespoons pastis*
*Freshly ground black pepper,*
*    to taste*
*6 dozen mussels*
*½ cup water*
*½ cup dry white wine*
*Lemon wedges for garnish*

1. Place the bread crumbs and hazelnuts in a food processor. Process until the nuts are very finely ground. Add the garlic and parsley and process again to combine well. Drizzle in the olive oil and *pastis*, pulsing the machine to moisten all evenly. Season the mixture with pepper and set aside.

2. Scrub the mussels under cold running water and beard them. Pour the water and the wine into a large pot. Add the mussels, cover, and cook over high heat just until the mussel shells open, about 5 minutes. Remove from the heat and let cool until easy to handle.

3. Remove and discard the top shell from each mussel, as well as any mussel that hasn't opened. Use a small knife to gently release the mussels from the shells, then nestle them back into the shells. The mussels may either be arranged on 6 individual gratin dishes or in rows on 1 large baking sheet. Using a small spoon or your hands, pat some of the bread crumb mixture lightly over each mussel to cover it completely. At this point, the mussels may be refrigerated for up to 4 hours before baking.

4. When ready to cook, preheat the oven to 475°F.

5. Bake the mussels until sizzling and golden brown, 5 to 7 minutes. Garnish with lemon wedges and serve at once.

Serves 6 as a luncheon or first course or 12 to 15 as an hors d'oeuvre

# HIGHLIGHTS OF A
# PROVENCE
## GETAWAY

the trip began, like Peter Mayle's *A Year in Provence,* with lunch. Earlier, *chez moi,* I had been counting my lucky stars, as I had been presented with the chance to cycle, in a nonguiding capacity, with the final Butterfield & Robinson tour of the 1994 season—the Provence Getaway—a four-day-long October spin through harvest-hued northern Provence. This trip length had been designed to lure cycle-hesitant or time-constrained folks with a rich preview of the delights of savoring the European countryside slowly by bicycle.

The tour began in late October, with our group of eighteen being carried by bus through the sprawling suburbs of Avignon and left motorless in the heart of Provence's most famous wine village, Châteauneuf-du-Pape. By noon of our first day we had yet to put sneaker to bicycle toe-clip to test the cycling waters, because tasting the wondrous wine from the majestic surrounding vineyards was much too diverting and irresistible.

We were at the Domaine du Pegaü, with filled glasses in hand and a welcoming cold lunch sprawled before us on platters lining the center of one long banquet table. As a group, we knew little about one another, but in the capable hands of our enthusiastic hostess, Laurence Féraud, we certainly were becoming knowledgeable about what makes the wines of Châteauneuf-du-Pape so special. There are hundreds of *père et fils* (father and son) wine-making pairs in France, but Laurence is part of a tiny minority of *père et fille,* or father and daughter, teams. She is proud of her wine and explained that the Domaine du Pegaü takes its name from the Provençal dialect for the fourteenth-century clay pitcher that was used for serving wine during the papal reign in Avignon. There are thirteen types of grapes authorized for the making of Châteauneuf-du-Pape wines, and Laurence and her *papa* cultivate eight of them. Some of the most coveted wines of Châteauneuf-du-Pape come from the revered vineyards of Beaucastel, Vieuxx Télégraphe, and Château Rayas, but the 1990 Féraud family reds have recently garnered rave reviews from the popular wine critic Robert Parker. Like being the first to invest in a great stock that is little known on Wall Street, it was as if we had stumbled serendipitously onto the inside track of the wine world.

Red Châteauneuf-du-Pape wines are characteristically meaty, jammy, concentrated, and alcoholic (at least 12.5 percent alcohol by law and up to a whopping 15 percent), due in part to a growing soil studded with large rounded pebbles, which store the heat of the sun-drenched Midi well into the night. The rocks also help the soil retain its moisture while increasing the sugar content of

*Châteauneuf~du~Pape*

the grapes to produce more alcohol in the wine. I, personally, have always been fondest of Châteauneuf-du-Pape's intriguing complexities as they are manifested in the lighter but very sophisticated white wines of the appellation. Far fewer white than red wines are produced, and since they are often hard to come by or quite expensive at home, I made a special point of fueling my precycling contemplations with Domaine du Pegaü's elegant and aromatic white wine. As a last thought, before ascending from cellar to cycle, I purchased two bottles of white and one of red as my first souvenirs of the trip.

Twenty-one-speed Trek *bicyclettes* greeted and reminded the group of the trip's raison d'être as we emerged two hours later from the depths of the wine cellar, leaving behind only the odd *tarte au chocolat* crumb. The bikes were all the same color—an appropriate cross between papal purple and the ruby of the now-familiar 1990 Domaine du Pegaü. I enjoyed this nifty nuance, but everyone else was eager to get started on the "wholesome" twenty-one-mile ride to our evening's destination, the splendid Hostellerie de Crillon-le-Brave, atop the sleepy little perched village of the same name. The trip that began with lunch now presented a ride that began with a hill out of Châteauneuf-du-Pape. Fortunately the same wine that had just combatted all the artery-clogging potential lurking in our luncheon *charcuterie* now made this climb relatively painless, but not so painless that anyone wanted to detour uphill for an extra 2 kilometers to view the crumbling ruins of the town's namesake summer papal château. Rather, we welcomed the heat radiating off the rocks in the vineyards on this crisp autumn day, and those deep breaths we took, disguising any shortness of breath, were filled with the just-noted scents of the afternoon wine: truffles and tar, sun-ripened fruit and spice, licorice, tannin, and tobacco. Life felt sublime, and the route even flattened out for several kilometers of very tranquil riding past golden fields and along narrow plane-tree-shaded lanes.

The first signs of another town appeared about an hour and

Domaine du Pégaï

Beaumes-de-Venise

Lou Castelet

a half later, as the speediest cyclists approached the terraced village of Beaumes-de-Venise. Surprise! We were back in wine country, in the village that gives its name to Provence's sweet muscat dessert wine. Most in the group were content to pause for a thirst-quenching Perrier at the town's roadside corner café, Lou Castelet. I, however, started thinking about how difficult it can be to find Muscat de Beaumes-de-Venise back in my neck of the New England woods, and my bicycle seemed to head instinctively for the local wine cooperative. I knew that later, when I was alone in the porterless, cartless train station in Avignon heading up to Paris to catch my transatlantic flight, I would briefly regret my penchant for purchasing such cumbersome souvenirs. But I also knew that once I was back in my Nantucket kitchen, recreating the inspiring tastes of my Provençal travels, I would be elated to have on hand select bottles brimming equally with grand wine and memories.

The seats back at the Lou Castelet café were wicker, sun-kissed, and filled with a bevy of cyclists. Amiable getting-acquainted conversations and embellished stories from the route were punctuated by rumors of the upcoming steep climb to the Hostellerie de Crillon-le-Brave. Some in the group began to think another round of Perriers followed by transport to the hotel in the company van sounded more like the vacation plan of their dreams. Because I had cycled and savored this route a few times before, I knew that I didn't want to miss out on pedaling the day's last scenic kilometers on a little back road whose shoulder is sometimes a cool, gurgling stream. I also always enjoyed cycling by the quaint bell-towered church in the tiny, in-between village of Caromb and then seeing both Crillon-le-Brave and Mont Ventoux looming in the distance. I persuaded a few in the group to head off with me and as we finally huffed and puffed our way up the tortuous Crillon hill, I concentrated only on how this strenuous stretch would afford me guiltless indulgence in the glistening black Nyons olives and creamy warm goat cheese toasts that always accompany apéritifs at the friendly Hostellerie.

Crillon-le-Brave is, at the very least, my favorite hotel in Provence's Vaucluse. Even if it weren't run by friend and former bicycle tour guide Peter Chittick (all guides eventually must face the reality that they cannot live by bicycle alone), I would still wax hyperbolic over its overflowing Pierre Deux country charm.

*Caromb*

*Crillon-le-Brave*

The common rooms are airy yet intimate, and what walls aren't softened by reams of gaily colored and patterned Souleiado fabrics are glazed in the muted gold, apricot, and terra-cotta tones of the surrounding countryside. This was now my fifth or sixth visit to the Hostellerie; each time I managed to stay in a different room, and each time I was most in love with my room-with-the-incredible-view of the moment. Peter spent three years lovingly and painstakingly converting this former private summer home into the present twenty-two-room retreat.

I sank with tired contentment into my room's warm bath, made all the more luxurious by aromatherapeutic splashes of the hotel's locally made *bain moussant*. Soon I was relaxed and ready to savor those dreamed-of luscious black olives, one by one, sip a refreshing spot of Côtes du Ventoux rosé, and then tuck myself and a few hungry companions cozily into one of the restaurant's stone-vaulted alcoves. Jean-David, the flamboyant young maître d' with the definitive handlebar mustache, arrived to indulge us with his recommendations on food and wine.

Fruit-studded desserts signaled the sweet end of this first magnificent day, and needless to say, no one wanted it to come to a close. Yet, already plans for day two were being discussed, a day promising a lazy route in the shadows (read: flat terrain) of the neighboring lacelike mountain range, the Dentelles de Montmirail. It dawned with plenty of warming sun, and the morning's leisurely pace afforded a chat-as-you-cycle time with fellow riders and local characters alike. There was also plenty of time to check out haphazard markets in the tiniest of villages, pose for photos in front of trickling tiered fountains, taste those grapes that had been left behind and ripened after the September harvest, and finally pack in a late-afternoon game of *pétanque*—accompanied by the obligatory shot of *pastis*—next to the imposing statue of Crillon-le-Brave himself (an apparently brave Renaissance hero).
The realization

*Hostellerie de Crillon-le-Brave*

that this was our group's second and last evening in Crillon-le-Brave seemed to heighten its seductive spell. At the same time, however, I was looking forward to the next day's ride, which was to take us via Vaison-la-Romaine, a town with both an ancient history of its own and a personal history for me, to Grignan, a town new to me in the lesser-traveled southern department of Drôme-Provençale. Crillon-le-Brave would be impossible to leave were it not for the incentive of a great coast downhill from the village to start the morning's cycling on an exhilarating note. The road to Vaison-la-Romaine was more trafficked than other roads we had been on, but then again, we had been spoiled. The outdoor market, near the midpoint of our morning ride, sprawled down the

*Dentelles de Montmirail*

one-street-town of Malaucène, and made up for the few extra cars encountered on the road. I stopped and bought a good year's supply of Provence's wonderful pastel soaps in scents of vanilla, lavender, almond, and rose. I also found some charming Provençal fabric and lace pillows filled with fragrant lavender blossoms. I bought a few, reasoning they would naturally cushion my bottles of wine when I packed, and make everything in my luggage smell of Provence.

Close to 11:30 A.M., my heart began to race as I approached Vaison-la-Romaine. A little over two years before, I had been leading a September cycling tour in Provence, with my group ending its weeklong adventure in Crillon-le-Brave. I had driven to Vaison-la-Romaine early in the morning to purchase a cele-

## Vaison-la-Romaine

### Malaucène

bration picnic for the group in the terrific Tuesday market. Just as I was loading the van with the last of the supplies, a huge crack of thunder sounded and the skies opened up. I started to head back toward Crillon-le-Brave in rains so blinding and winds so fierce that I was forced to pull off the road. I became a bit panicky and began talking to myself, asking what was more important: my life or the group's picnic. I opted for the picnic. A combination of luck and reckless determination got me back to the hotel, where I began ferrying the frustrated cyclists to our picnic site, now moved from the vineyards into our host's rustic *grenier.* Just as I was getting ready to prepare the picnic's *pièce de résistance,* the still-violent storm caused the *grenier's* jerry-built electricity to fail. An *aïoli* whisked in pitch dark, however, managed to be just as rich and pungent, and even a mite more memorable, than all those made over the years under a perfect noonday sun.

The return visit now brought a thankfully dry tour of the town's namesake excavations revealing a Roman villa, street, and basilica. Soon, however, the long afternoon ride to Grignan beckoned. This was the longest riding day of the trip, but the scenery was so spectacular as to be energizing. There were olive trees laden with fruit holding on for the last few weeks of ripening and plumping before November's harvest. There were acres on end of long-ago-picked-yet-still-aromatic lavender fields. And the reds, russets, and golds of the autumn vineyards and orchards were dazzlingly luminous. I honestly could not recall ever biking in a more beautiful and unspoiled area of France.

The encroaching coolness of the late afternoon and the impending sunset made the fading last blossoms in the spectacular gardens surrounding our Grignan hotel, La Roseraie, a welcome sight. La Roseraie, with its grand stone staircases and balconies, is an imposing building from the outside. The rooms inside are soaring and spacious but dotted with that questionable style of rural French decorative accents that can be cause for a chuckle or two while cycling and musing over collective experiences. Nonetheless, I was excited to be here and looked forward to our tour of the Château de Grignan the following morning. The town's landmark château had been built in the Middle Ages on top of a rock resembling an acropolis and overlooking the village.

*Grignan*

Rebuilding during the sixteenth century transformed it into a fine Renaissance château, but it was the presence of the famous letter writer Madame de Sévigné that turned the château into a true historic site.

Some château tours

*Château de Grignan*

can deliver a lethal dose of ennui, but the one in Grignan proved to be lively, awe-inspiring, and enlightening—a fabulous cultural beginning to the last day of our Provence getaway. We descended from the Château de Grignan feeling like royalty on bicycles and hit the road toward Nyons, the olive center of Provence. The cycling was just as breathtaking in its rural isolation as the previous day's route. The lavender fields seemed to stretch on forever. We cycled into the plains beneath the protective ring of mountains that give Nyons a microclimate so conducive to the cultivation of olives. I remembered reading the legend of St. Caesarius, who scooped up a handful of mild ocean air and delivered its gentleness to Nyons, where it has flourished through the centuries.

As I amused myself with this lovely tale, something not so wonderful befell my trusty purple bicycle: a flat tire. Being the mechanically challenged person that I am, I counted my lucky lavender fields that I just happened to be biking in the company of an engineer, a meteorologist, and a businessman. The businessman meant well, but it was the husband and wife team of engineer and meterologist who became my true saviors. Triumphant, we biked a few kilometers further and then paused to celebrate with some sweet roadside grapes and to snap a few photos. Pedaling on, my same tire soon became flat again. I began to wonder if there was some hidden significance to the fact that in all my years of cycling abroad, my only flats had occurred in Provence. It was determined that I had a defective tire with a maladjusted spoke puncturing my inner tube. My spirits were deflated along with my tire, but the engineer devised a brilliant padded patch and we were en route once again. Unfortunately, the delays had made us late for our scheduled midday rendezvous

Nyons

with the rest of our group. When we at last arrived, an hour late, we found the rest of our companions reveling in a feast atop a rocky perch overlooking Nyons's olive groves.

Laura, half of the group's guiding team, had laid out an incredible picnic, replete with patterned Provençal tablecloths, olives galore, roast chickens, rich cheeses, bouquets of baguettes, and a sampling of regional wines along with the omnipresent bottle of *pastis*. I knew I was either in heaven or Provence, because my flat-tire saga managed to end with lunch!

The last few kilometers into the town of Nyons served as a soothing *digestif* after such ravenous feasting. All of our group's olive aficionados piled into the Cooperative Agricole du Nyonsais for an olive-buying frenzy. I spotted *Les olives du soleil dans la cuisine,* an entire book devoted to the olive cookery of this sun-drenched region. I also purchased my most precious and portable culinary souvenir of the trip: two tiny jars of black truffles from the Vaucluse. The truffles actually looked like a pair of Nyons olives in quarantine, but the triple-digit francs on the jar were a surefire indication of the contents.

The evening at our hotel back in Grignan brought, of course, a festive, toast-filled farewell banquet. But facing the end of this Provence getaway seemed  too sad to contemplate or write about. Better to say a fond *au revoir* in Nyons, where silvery green olive branches, century-old symbols of peace, grow for panoramic miles around.

# SUPPERS OF LAMB AND OTHER FINE FARE

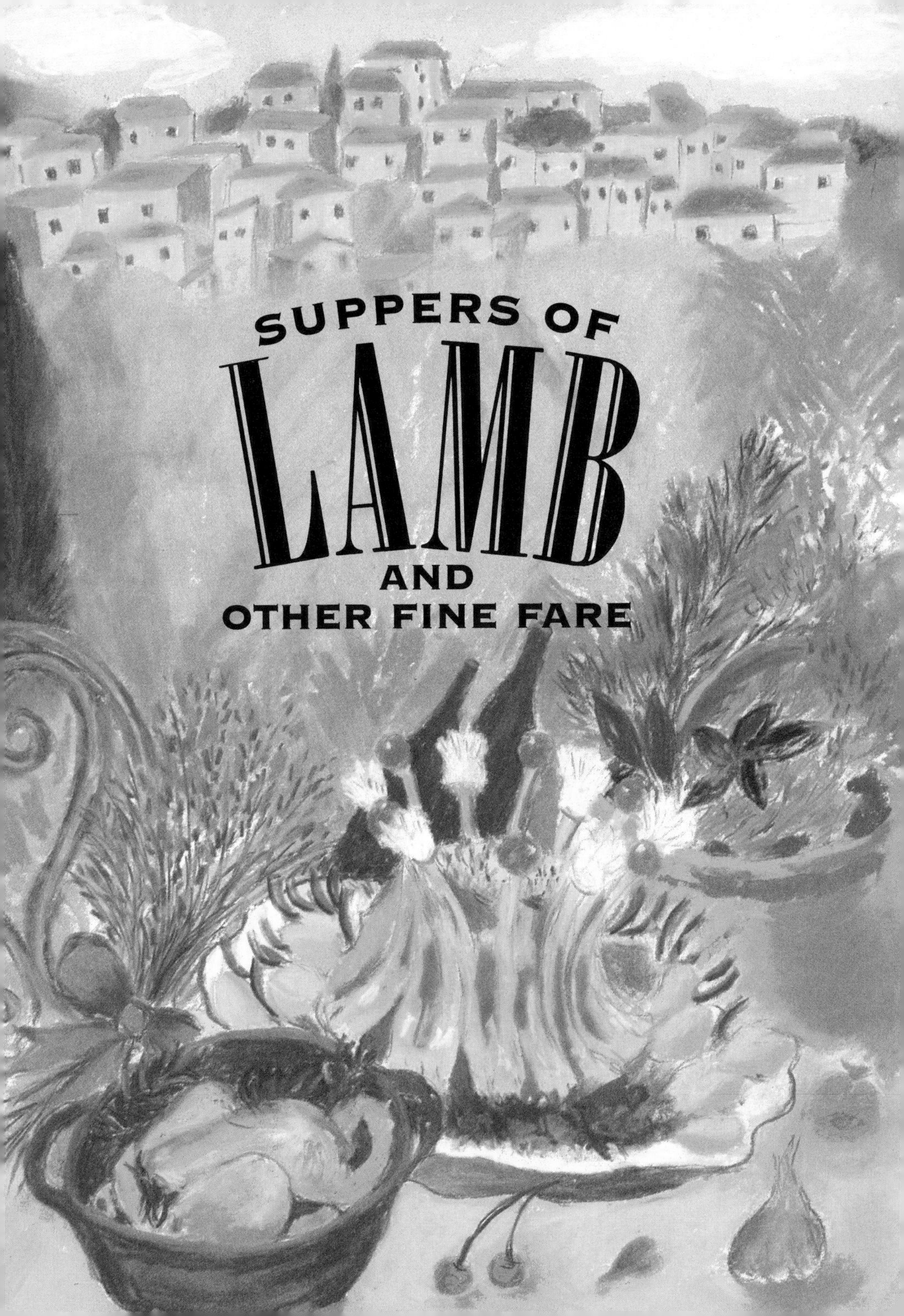

Provence's colorful and healthful cuisine may be based primarily on vegetables, but this blessed province is, after all, still a part of France, and the French indisputably love meat. The meat of choice in Provence just so happens to be some of the most highly regarded in all of France—the succulent Sisteron lamb, raised on the wild rosemary, thyme, and savory that blankets the rugged hills of Haute Provence.

Many are the suppers of lamb we cyclists enjoy while pedaling the backroads of inland Provence. In all honesty, it is hard not to experience cravings for this prized local meat when pedaling can often make a cyclist end up smelling like a perfectly roasted leg of lamb! For, a typical day of bicycling in Provence includes riding underneath a sun blazing and brazen enough to extract perspiration redolent of the previous evening's garlicky cuisine, which then mingles with the arid *garrigue* scent of wild rosemary, so pervasive at times as to be mistaken for the exhilarating fragrance of vast blue sky. Add in the rich red wine vineyards of Châteauneuf-du-Pape, Gigondas, and Vacqueyras as *dégustation* destinations, and the whole day can be ridden as one glorious outdoor preview of savors to be harmonized anew in the evening's offering of *gigot à la Provençale*. Best enjoyed, of course, after a long and restorative bath or shower!

Neither the pedalers on my trips nor the Provençaux choose to live by lamb alone, however. *Daubes,* rich and long-simmered meat stews, are the favored antidote to the frightfully raw and relentless stretches of *mistral* visitation. Chicken, as one might well expect, is bathed in countless cloves of garlic or napped with bright red tomatoes, while rabbit is splashed with the region's favorite sip, *pastis,* and duck and pork combine spectacularly with the countryside's celebrated apricots and olives.

# provençal Leg of Lamb with roasted red pepper sauce

Lots of people unintentionally roast a leg of lamb the way it is typically done in Provence—with garlic and rosemary. What makes this recipe different is that little pieces of anchovy are nestled into the slits along with the garlic, and the rosemary is used with sheer abandon. The robust flavors are completed by flambéing the rosemary after the lamb has finished roasting and then deglazing the pan with red wine and a roasted pepper purée to make a tasty accompanying sauce.

Although a leg of lamb is not considered nearly as elegant as a rack or thick chops, I think it always makes a Sunday evening dinner simultaneously festive and homey.

1 leg of lamb (6 to 7 pounds), fell removed, leg trimmed of
   all but a few thin patches of fat
4 large cloves garlic, peeled and cut into thin slivers
1 can (2 ounces) flat anchovies, drained
2 fat bunches fresh rosemary (about 8 cups loosely packed)
3 tablespoons olive oil
Sea or coarse salt and freshly ground black pepper, to taste

ROASTED RED PEPPER PURÉE
4 roasted bell peppers (see Box, facing page)
1½ tablespoons olive oil
3 cloves garlic, minced
Sea or coarse salt and freshly ground black pepper, to taste
½ cup dry red wine

134

1. The day before you plan to roast the lamb, cut random 1-inch-deep slits all over the leg by inserting the tip of a sharp paring knife into the meat. Insert the garlic slivers. Cut the anchovies into ½-inch lengths and insert them alongside the garlic. Break off several little sprigs from the rosemary and insert them into the slits as well. Rub the olive oil all over the lamb, season with salt and pepper, cover with plastic wrap, and refrigerate overnight.

2. Make the red pepper purée: Cut the roasted red peppers into 1-inch pieces and place them in a food processor. Heat the olive oil in a small skillet over medium heat, add the garlic, and sauté just until softened, 1 to 2 minutes. Combine with the peppers in the processor and process all until smooth. Season the purée with salt and pepper and store, covered, in the refrigerator until ready to use.

3. When ready to cook the lamb, bring it and the red pepper purée to room temperature. Preheat the oven to 450°F.

4. Lay half of the remaining rosemary over the center of a large flameproof roasting pan. Place the leg of lamb on a roasting rack

over the rosemary. Lay the remaining rosemary over the top of the lamb. Roast for 20 minutes and then reduce the heat to 350°F. Continue cooking until a meat thermometer inserted into the center of the lamb registers 130°F (for medium-rare meat), 1¼ to 1½ hours. Remove it from the oven. Standing back, carefully light it with a long kitchen match to flambé the rosemary on top of the lamb and let it burn out. Remove the lamb to a cutting board, discarding all the charred rosemary remains, and let it rest while making the sauce.

5. To make the sauce, remove and discard any large rosemary stems remaining in the bottom of the roasting pan. Place the pan on two stove burners over medium heat. Pour in the wine and stir with a wooden spoon to loosen any brown bits clinging to the bottom of the pan. Add the pepper purée and stir to make a smooth sauce. Let the sauce simmer, stirring occasionally, for 10 minutes.

6. Carve the leg of lamb into thin slices. Nap each serving of the lamb with some of the roasted red pepper sauce and serve at once.

135

Makes 6 to 8 servings

## ROASTED BELL PEPPERS

To roast bell peppers, preheat the broiler. Place the peppers in an aluminum foil-lined roasting pan and broil them, a few inches from the heat, turning frequently, until they are blistered and charred all over, 10 to 12 minutes. Transfer the hot peppers to a plastic bag and seal it by loosely knotting the top. When the peppers are cool enough to handle, remove them from the bag, peel away the skins, and discard the stems and seeds.

# butterflied Leg of Lamb

〜

**t**he marinade for this grilled, butterflied leg of lamb has many of the rich flavors of Provençal cuisine—lots of garlic, anchovies, olive oil, *herbes de Provence,* and red wine—and it never fails to garner absolutely ecstatic reviews. I'm additionally fond of the recipe as one that should be dedicated to my cyclists because the Butterfield & Robinson bike-tour company is referred to through-out France as "Butterfly" by the French, who can never seem to say or remember its real name.

136

I frequently serve the butterflied lamb hot off the grill, with-out a sauce, but if it is early autumn and time to harvest grapes, I find it hard to resist making an accompanying wild grape and mint sauce. My late-September bicycle rides on Nantucket usu-ally result in a carefully balanced basket filled with the island's wild Concord grapes, but any dark-skinned grape, whether plucked from native or foreign vines, may be used in the sauce.

MARINADE
5 cloves garlic, minced
3 tablespoons anchovy paste
½ cup minced fresh parsley
2 tablespoons herbes de Provence
2 teaspoons freshly ground black pepper
¼ cup olive oil
1¼ cups dry red wine
1 leg of lamb (6 to 7 pounds), boned and butterflied
Several sprigs of fresh rosemary

WILD GRAPE AND MINT SAUCE (OPTIONAL)
3 tablespoons Consorzio rosemary oil, or regular olive oil
2 medium red onions, cut into ½-inch-wide crescent slivers
2 pounds dark-skinned grapes, halved and seeded
½ cup golden raisins
½ cup dry red wine
2½ tablespoons honey
⅓ cup cassis
½ cup chopped fresh mint

137

1. The morning of the day you plan to serve the lamb, make the marinade. Place the garlic, anchovy paste, parsley, *herbes de Provence,* pepper, and olive oil in a food processor and process until smooth. With the machine running, pour the wine through the feed tube to thin the marinade. Lay the lamb out flat in a large, shallow glass dish and cover with the marinade. Dot with the rosemary sprigs, cover, and let marinate, in the refrigerator for at least 6 hours, turning the lamb a few times.

2. Make the wild grape and mint sauce, if using. Heat the oil over medium-high heat in a medium-size saucepan. Add the onions and sauté until quite soft and just beginning to turn color, 12 to 15

minutes. Stir in the grapes, raisins, red wine, honey, and cassis. Bring to a boil and then reduce the heat and simmer until the grapes just begin to collapse, 5 to 7 minutes. Refrigerate, covered, until ready to serve. Just before serving, reheat the sauce over low heat and stir in the mint.

3. Remove the lamb from the refrigerator and allow it to come to room temperature.

4. Meanwhile, prepare charcoal for grilling. (If grapevines are available, they are excellent added to the fire.)

5. When the coals are hot, place the lamb on the grill about 4 inches from the heat. Grill, basting with any extra marinade, 15 to 20 minutes per side for medium-rare meat. Carve the lamb into thin slices and serve as is or nap with the warm grape sauce.

Makes 8 to 10 servings

138

# roast rack of Lamb with Lavender Honey and Herbes de provence

Sure, it's tempting fate to tuck glass jars of honey spied at some little hilltop village's weekly open-air market into the ever-jiggling handlebar pack on my bike, but Provence's lavender honey is simply too delicious to leave behind and too difficult to find at home. I can't help the fact that Lavender Honey Ice Cream (see Index) is my current addiction or that this recipe has become my all-time favorite way to prepare elegant racks of lamb.

Provence's lavender honey (*miel de lavande*) has the creamy color and texture of our churned honeys, combined with an herbaceous and slightly floral undertone of purple lavender flowers. The last jars I purchased boasted of enough vitamin and mineral richness to make the honey a health *"élément par excellence"*— certainly an attribute that can assuage any guilt stemming from indulging in red meat or ice cream.

If you're not fortunate enough to have a private stash of lavender honey, substitute clover or another wildflower honey of choice in this recipe, but try to use an *herbes de Provence* blend that contains a few lavender flowers.

1 cup fresh French bread crumbs
2½ tablespoons *herbes de Provence*
2 teaspoons freshly ground
    black pepper
1 teaspoon sea or coarse salt
2½ tablespoons fruity olive oil
2 racks of lamb (about 1½ pounds
    each), fully trimmed and
    "frenched" (see Box, page 140)
⅓ to ½ cup lavender honey, or another honey of choice

139

1. Preheat the oven to 450°F.

2. Combine the bread crumbs with the *herbes de Provence*, pepper, and salt. Moisten the mixture with the olive oil and set aside.

3. Season the racks of lamb with additional salt and pepper and arrange, meat side up, in a roasting pan. Roast for 12 minutes. Remove from the oven and coat each rack all over with a thin layer of honey. Sprinkle with a generous layer of the bread crumb mixture, pressing

gently to make it adhere to the honey-coated meat. Return the racks to the oven and continue roasting another 10 to 15 minutes for medium-rare meat.

4. Let the lamb rest 5 to 10 minutes before carving. Using a sharp knife, cut the racks between the bones into individual chops. Serve 2 to 3 chops per person.

Makes 4 to 6 servings

## FRENCHING RACKS OF LAMB

A rack of lamb is the whole wonderfully succulent rib-chop section from one side of the animal. Such succulence, however, is not arrived at easily. Racks are covered with a great deal of fat that must be trimmed away before roasting. I usually ask my butcher to trim and "french" my racks of lamb, but occasionally I end up having to "french" my own racks.

Frenching is actually a very elegant-sounding term for removing the not-very-elegant fat that is webbed in between the seven or eight ribs of the rack. To remove the fat, use a sharp pairing or boning knife to cut straight down between the rib bones, running the knife from the top of each rib bone down to the solid, meaty beginning of the rack's loin meat. Then make a half-inch horizontal cut between the ribs along the meaty top of the rack in order to facilitate removing the fat in an elongated U-shaped piece. Once the fat is removed from between all the ribs in this manner, scrape the bones to remove any bits of fat still clinging to them. The rack is now officially "frenched."

# grilled ∫houlder LAmb chop∫

L amb chops grilled over the embers of a wood fire are beloved in Provence. While thick loin lamb chops may certainly be prepared in this manner, I've grown fond of using the more economical but mighty tasty shoulder cut of chop in this simple but favorite recipe. The meat may also be broiled indoors if time or weather prevents firing up the outdoor grill. Serve the chops with Olive-Smashed Potatoes (see Index), Minted Swiss Chard with Red Onion and Sopressetta (see Index), and a light and affordable red wine from the Côtes du Rhone or Côtes du Lubéron for a satisfying weekday dinner.

141

*6 shoulder lamb chops, 8 to 10*
  *ounces each*
*2½ tablespoons olive oil*
*2½ tablespoons herbes de*
  *Provence*
*Freshly ground black pepper*
*Sea or coarse salt*

1. Lay the chops out on a platter; brush both sides lightly with olive oil. Sprinkle both sides generously and evenly with the *herbes de Provence;* season with the pepper. Let marinate at room temperature for 30 minutes to 1 hour.

2. Prepare charcoal for grilling or preheat the broiler.

3. Season the chops with salt and grill or broil them 4 to 5 inches from the heat, 3 to 4 minutes per side for medium-rare meat. Serve at once.

Makes 6 servings

# Late-summer tian of eggplant, squash, tomatoes, and Lamb

In Provence, layered vegetable gratins are called *tians,* after the round or oval earthenware dishes in which they are baked. Greens such as Swiss chard, spinach, and sorrel are often mixed with cooked rice and eggs to make one sort of *tian,* but I'm partial to those that combine vegetables found in ratatouille, such as eggplant, squash, and tomatoes. Ground lamb has been added to that threesome in this *tian* to make for a dish hearty enough to take center stage at a homey, late-summer dinner. A basket of Pain Provençal (see Index), a mesclun salad, and a bottle or two of simple rosé or red wine are all that's needed to complete the meal with Provençal panache.

2 medium eggplants, stemmed and sliced into
     ½-inch-thick rounds
Sea or coarse salt
3 large yellow squash, stemmed and sliced into
     ½-inch-thick rounds
¼ cup plus 3 tablespoons olive oil
3 tablespoons herbes de Provence
Freshly ground black pepper, to taste
1 large onion, diced
3 cloves garlic, minced
1 pound lean ground lamb
½ cup dry red wine
½ cup slivered fresh basil
1 cup freshly grated Parmesan or Gruyère cheese
4 large vine-ripened tomatoes, sliced ½-inch thick

TOPPING
1 cup fresh French bread crumbs
½ cup minced fresh parsley
2 tablespoons slivered fresh basil
⅓ cup freshly grated Parmesan cheese
3 tablespoons olive oil

1. Layer the eggplant slices in a colander, sprinkling them generously with salt as you go; allow to drain for 30 minutes.

2. Preheat the oven to 375°F.

3. Rinse the eggplant slices and pat them dry. Lay out both the eggplant and squash rounds in a single layer on large baking sheets. Brush them lightly on one side with ¼ cup of the olive oil. Sprinkle the vegetables generously with the *herbes de Provence* and season with pepper. Bake the vegetables until softened and just beginning to brown, 15 to 20 minutes.

4. Meanwhile, heat the remaining 3 tablespoons olive oil in a large skillet over medium-high heat. Add the onion and garlic and sauté until softened, about 5 minutes. Add the lamb and cook, crumbling it into small bits with the back of a wooden spoon, until it loses its pink color, 7 to 8 minutes. Pour in the wine and continue cooking until the wine has reduced by half, 5 to 7 minutes more. Season the mixture with salt and pepper, stir in the basil, and remove from the heat.

5. Assemble the *tian* in a gratin dish that is 12 to 14 inches wide. Make a layer of half of the eggplant rounds and sprinkle lightly with about 2 tablespoons of the grated cheese. Top with a layer of half of the squash rounds and sprinkle them with cheese as well. Next, spread half of the lamb mixture over the squash rounds, and then top with half of the tomato slices. Sprinkle the tomatoes with 2 more tablespoons grated cheese, and then repeat the layering process all over again with the remaining vegetables and meat. The *tian* should end with a final layer of tomatoes.

144

6. Make the topping: Combine the bread crumbs, parsley, basil, and Parmesan in a small bowl. Moisten the mixture with the olive oil and then sprinkle it evenly over the top of the *tian*. Cover the *tian* tightly with aluminum foil and bake for 30 minutes. Uncover and continue baking until the vegetables are very tender and the top is crusted brown, 30 to 45 minutes longer. Let the *tian* cool for a few minutes and then serve by scooping it out onto plates.

makes 6 servings

# demi-daube

∞

d*aube* is the French name for a hearty stew often made from guarded family recipes and cooked over the embers of a fire in a sealed earthenware casserole. While not first-choice fare for fueling our mild and sunny spring and fall days of cycling in Provence, this is the dish to savor after an encounter with Provence's dreaded and fierce *mistral* wind or to prepare back home when hunkering down for winter's worst. Since cattle do not graze in the fragrant fields of Provence, it is thought that beef *daubes* came into being as a means of tenderizing the tough meat of the vanquished bulls after bullfights in the Carmargue. While watching bullfights remains a popular summer amusement throughout the Midi, *daubes* have thankfully evolved to include more enticing cuts of beef.

Since I recall reading somewhere the French edict "A *daube* is not a *daube* unless it has marinated for at least six hours and then cooked for at least another six hours," I feared offending some authority in calling this robust facsimile a *daube*. Having a recipe that matches the marinating criterion but meets the cooking time only halfway, with three hours of simmering, seemed logically to dictate the playful name of *demi-daube*.

In Avignon, in particular, it is customary to accompany a *daube* with a macaroni gratin moistened with aromatic cooking juices from the stewing meat, and a poetically licensed gratin recipe follows this one. In addition to bone-chilling weather, a *daube* or *demi-daube* dinner is best complemented by a bountiful green salad and bottle or two of a big, chewy red Rhône wine, such as Crozes-Hermitage, Côte-Rôtie, or Châteauneuf-du-Pape.

145

4 pounds boneless sirloin steak, ¾ to 1 inch thick
2 tablespoons herbes de Provence
1 tablespoon freshly ground black pepper
½ cup plus 3 tablespoons fruity olive oil
10 cloves garlic, minced
2 large onions, coarsely chopped
2 tablespoons julienned orange zest
¾ cup balsamic or red wine vinegar
1¾ cups dry red wine
Sea or coarse salt, to taste
8 anchovy fillets, drained
3 tablespoons all-purpose flour
½ cup drained capers
Revamped Pasta Gratin (recipe follows)
Minced fresh parsley, for garnish

146

1. Trim the fat from the sirloin and cut the meat into 8 fairly equal portions. Combine the *herbes de Provence* with the pepper and then rub the mixture evenly over both sides of the pieces of meat. Place the meat in a single layer in a shallow glass dish. Pour ½ cup of the olive oil over it and sprinkle with half the minced garlic. Marinate the meat, covered, in the refrigerator, turning occasionally, for at least 6 hours or overnight.

2. Preheat the oven to 300°F.

3. Combine the onions and orange zest with the rest of the minced garlic. Remove the meat from the marinade, reserving the liquid. Scatter one-third of the onion mixture over the bottom of an ovenproof 4-quart casserole or Dutch oven. Arrange 4 pieces of the meat on top, and then sprinkle with another third of the onion mix. Repeat the process once more with another layer of meat and a final layer of onions.

4. Pour the reserved marinade into the casserole, along with

## HERBES DE PROVENCE

When people initially describe Provence, they most often talk of the extraordinary light that bathes the land in combination with fragrances of wild hillside herbs that permeate the air. The light is not transportable, but the aromas are in the form of pouches of the dried *herbes de Provence,* sold as souvenirs literally everywhere in Provence. These commercial blends usually contain thyme, rosemary, marjoram, oregano, basil, and savory and are often packed in pretty cloth sacs decorated with Provençal patterns. Curiously enough, most blends sold in Provence do not contain lavender flowers because it has never been the native custom to use lavender as a cooking herb. I personally love the taste of a little lavender in many of my Provençal recipes and therefore endorse using the lavender-speckled *herbes de Provence*-style mixtures sold by two American companies: Morton & Bassett of San Francisco and Nantucket Off-Shore Seasonings, whose blend is marketed as Mt. Olympus Rub. Simply seasoning fish, chicken, or lamb with aromatic *herbes de Provence* before grilling or roasting makes for a quick, easy, and delectable method of bringing the famous savors of Provence to any doorstep.

the vinegar and 1 cup of the wine. Season conservatively with salt, bearing in mind that anchovies and capers will be adding salty flavor to the stew later on. Cover the *daube* tightly and bake for 3 hours, giving a stir to all every hour or so. (If you are making the pasta gratin, ladle out 1 cup of cooking liquid after 2 hours.)

5. To finish the *daube,* mince the anchovies finely and then mash them with the remaining 3 tablespoons olive oil; set aside briefly. Remove the meat from the casserole and keep warm on a separate

147

platter. Place the casserole on the stove over medium-low heat. Put the flour in a small sieve and sift it over the cooking juices in the casserole. Then pour in the remaining ¾ cup wine. Whisk constantly until thickened, 5 to 7 minutes. Add the anchovy mixture and cook 1 to 2 minutes more. Return the meat to the casserole and stir in the capers. Serve at once or keep warm over low heat until ready to serve. Accompany each serving with a scoop of the Revamped Pasta Gratin and garnish all with a sprinkling of parsley.

makes 6 to 8 servings

# revamped pasta gratin

All the bicycling tours I lead in Provence share a rendezvous point in the lively city of Avignon. Most participants arrive a day or two in advance in order to visit the magnificent Palace of the Popes, the imposing remains of the fourteenth-century papal residence built as a refuge from the anarchy in Rome. Such pious sightseeing inevitably breeds a need for some rebellious materialism, and, fortunately, present-day Avignon abounds in shops selling regional pottery, perfumes, fabrics, and clothing. The combination of sightseeing with shopping can in turn work up a healthy appetite, and many in my groups tend to book an evening table at the restaurant La Fourchette, having read in one guidebook or another about its supposedly marvelous *daube de boeuf à l'Avignonnaise* and macaroni gratin.

I mention these particulars because over the years many disappointed diners have greeted me with the dismay of having traveled all the way to Provence to dine on specialties resembling American beef stew and macaroni and cheese! I'm always most sympathetic to their disgruntlement over the traditional macaroni gratin and am happy finally to be of service in offering my take on pasta gratin for home consumption. Orecchiette is my preferred shape of pasta, and the gratin is further enhanced by the creamy addition of tangy goat cheese. Do keep in mind that the recipe is intended to be made along with the *Demi-Daube* and will require some of its meat juices.

1 pound orecchiette pasta
1½ cups heavy (or whipping) cream
1½ cups light cream or half-and-half
8 ounces creamy goat cheese
1 cup juices from the Demi-Daube (page 145)
Sea or coarse salt and freshly ground black pepper, to taste
Pinch of freshly ground nutmeg

149

CRUMB TOPPING
1½ cups fresh French bread crumbs
2 cloves garlic, minced
2 tablespoons olive oil
½ cup minced fresh parsley
½ cup freshly grated Parmesan cheese

1. If you are cooking the *Demi-Daube*, your oven should already be preheated to 300°F. At least 1 hour before the *daube* is scheduled to come out of the oven, bring a large pot of salted water to a boil and cook the orecchiette until *al dente.* Drain well and transfer the pasta to a large mixing bowl.

2. Meanwhile, combine the heavy and light creams with the goat cheese in a saucepan and heat over medium heat, stirring to

melt the cheese. When the sauce is completely smooth, combine it with the pasta. Add the juices from the *Demi-Daube* (ladled out after the *daube* has cooked for 2 hours) and stir into the pasta as well. Season all to taste with salt, pepper, and a pinch of nutmeg. Transfer the pasta to a large (2½- to 3-quart) buttered gratin dish.

3. Make the crumb topping: Combine all the ingredients in a small bowl, and then sprinkle the mixture evenly over the top of the gratin. Bake the gratin alongside the *daube* until well heated, 30 to 40 minutes.

4. Just before serving, preheat the broiler and broil the gratin, 4 to 5 inches from the heat, until the crumb topping becomes crusty and golden brown, 2 to 3 minutes. Serve at once.

makes 8 rich and ample servings

# grilled skirt steak with anchovy-olive butter

As much as I appreciate the many ways in which lamb is cooked and celebrated throughout Provence, every once in a while I feel the urge to satisfy my carnivorous yearnings with the less gamy flavor of another red meat. When that craving for beef strikes, I see not the precious, rosy morsel of tenderloin always so carefully arranged and meted out at fancy Riviera dining temples but rather the more rustic and wonderfully tasty bistro-style steak known as *onglet*.

Often in Provence, *onglet* will be simply but deliciously grilled with a generous sprinkling of *herbes de Provence,* but if the chef is in a more creative mood, the meat may be topped with a smear of silky black tapenade or a melting dollop of anchovy butter. I'm especially partial to the butter embellishment, as its taste comes as a welcome, almost exotic treat in the midst of a cuisine so devoted to olive oil.

At home, I have achieved results worthy of my fondest Provençal memories by grilling skirt steak—that once economical and still succulent cut of beef put on the American map by lovers of sizzling Tex-Mex fajitas. If skirt steak happens to be difficult to find, flank steak may be substituted. Actually, truth be told, I'd probably find almost any food that lends itself readily to grilling absolutely sublime when topped with this lip-smacking anchovy-olive butter.

One final note on the butter: It will look particularly appetizing if blended with the purple flowers from blossoming thyme. Regular thyme leaves, however, will add the same flavor, if not the same subtle beauty.

151

*1 skirt steak (about 2 pounds)*
*3 tablespoons olive oil*
*2 tablespoons herbes de Provence*
*Sea or coarse salt, to taste*

ANCHOVY-OLIVE BUTTER
*8 tablespoons (1 stick) unsalted butter, at room temperature*
*8 anchovy fillets, drained and coarsely chopped*
*¼ cup imported black olives, pitted and coarsely*
    *chopped*
*1½ teaspoons fresh thyme blossoms or leaves, removed*
    *from the stem*

1. Prepare charcoal for grilling.

2. Place the steak on a platter and rub it on both sides with the olive oil. Sprinkle evenly on both sides with the *herbes de Provence* and some salt; let stand for 10 to 15 minutes.

3. Meanwhile, make the anchovy-olive butter: Place the butter in a small bowl and use a fork to mash the anchovies, olives, and thyme into it. The butter should be coarsely textured rather than well blended and homogeneous.

4. When the charcoals are ready, grill the steak 3 to 4 inches from the coals for roughly 3 to 4 minutes per side for rare to medium-rare meat. Divide the steak into four serving portions and top each immediately with a generous dollop of the anchovy-olive butter. Serve at once.

Makes 4 servings

152

**Note:** If using flank steak, it should be thinly sliced and fanned onto the serving plates before dotting with the butter. Any leftover butter will keep in the refrigerator for 1½ to 2 weeks.

# pork and apricot ragoût

As I've noted before, the first meal savored on foreign soil often lingers the longest in memory. I had just flown across the Atlantic and then caught the high-speed train from Paris's Gare de Lyon to Butterfield & Robinson's headquarters in Burgundy in order to rendezvous with my British co-guide, Jonathan Green, for our upcoming September bicycle tour in Provence. I was feeling understandably jet-lagged and left the driving of our noisy, power-steeringless, diesel luggage-transporting van to Jonathan for the long, late-afternoon haul from Beaune to the South of France. I awoke from a sound snooze around 9:30 P.M., just as we were passing by the Arc de Triomphe in Orange, where we had agreed to stop for the first night of our preguiding venture. After checking into a funky little hotel with strangely angled but somehow charming rooms, we went in search of a meal.

It didn't take long to find ourselves ensconced underneath a big tree at a dreamy streetside table, with both red wine and getting-acquainted conversation flowing. The immediate ambience, abetted by another bottle or two of wine, and the unmistakably Provençal taste of sweet apricots and pungent olives in my restorative serving of pork ragoût took us way past midnight and naturally set the stage for what my exuberantly English co-guide would term a "brilliant" trip.

153

2 tablespoons olive oil
2 ounces pancetta or bacon, diced
2 pounds lean pork, cut into ¾-inch cubes
1 medium onion, minced
3 cloves garlic, minced
2 cups dry white wine
2½ tablespoons tomato paste
2 tablespoons slivered fresh sage or 1 tablespoon dried, crumbled
Sea or coarse salt and freshly ground black pepper, to taste
⅔ cup pitted and halved imported green olives
½ cup coarsely chopped dried apricots
Rosé Rice (page 200), for serving

1. Heat the olive oil over medium-high heat in a Dutch oven or large stew pot. Add the pancetta and cook until crisp, 6 to 8 minutes.

Remove from the pot with a slotted spatula and set aside to drain on paper towels. Add the pork to the fat remaining in the pot and sear until browned on all sides, 5 to 7 minutes. Remove from the pot and set aside temporarily.

2. Add the onion and garlic to the pot and sauté until softened, 2 to 3 minutes. Pour in the white wine, and then stir in the tomato paste to blend well. Season with the sage, salt, and pepper. Add the seared pork and any accumulated juices to the pot. Cover and simmer, stirring occasionally, for 1¼ hours.

3. Add the olives and apricots to the ragoût, cover again, and continue simmering for another 30 minutes. Just before serving, sprinkle the ragoût with the reserved pancetta. Serve hot accompanied by Rosé Rice.

Makes 4 servings

# roasted pork Loin scented with white wine and aniseeds

While sage is traditionally paired with pork in Provence, this recipe exalts a delicious merger with another of the region's favored seasonings: anise. The original inspiration for roasting pork with aniseeds comes from Caprilands Herb Farm, in Connecticut, but the herby bread crumb stuffing is typically Provençal, with the exception of the dried cherries, which I added to recall the trail of cherry pits that often mark my route when I am pedaling through the orchards of the Vaucluse in late May. The pork is slowly roasted in a moisturizing bath of white wine to ensure melt-in-your-moth succulence. The roast makes a splendid entrée for dinner in the countryside, whether the environs are the Litchfield hills of Connecticut or the lavender fields of the Lubéron.

1½ cups dry white wine
2 tablespoons aniseeds
¼ cup olive oil
1 medium onion, minced
1 teaspoon dried thyme
2 teaspoons dried marjoram
2½ cups French bread crumbs, made from day-old
    bread
½ cup dried cherries
Sea or coarse salt and freshly ground black pepper,
    to taste
1 pork loin (4 to 5 pounds), butterflied

l. Preheat the oven to 300°F. Line a roasting pan with a large sheet of heavy-duty aluminum foil.

2. Combine the wine and aniseeds in a small saucepan and bring to a simmer over medium heat. Let simmer a few minutes and then remove from the heat.

3. Heat the oil in a skillet over medium heat. Add the onion, thyme, and marjoram and sauté until the onion is soft, 5 to 7 minutes. Add the bread crumbs, and cherries; continue cooking until the

crumbs are lightly browned, 7 to 10 minutes. Season with salt and pepper. Remove from the heat.

4. Spread the bread crumb mixture evenly over the butterflied pork loin and then roll the pork, like a jelly roll, back into its original shape. Secure the loin by tying it at intervals with kitchen string. Place the pork in the center of the prepared pan and bring the foil loosely up around the sides of the roast. Spoon the wine and aniseed mixture over and around the pork. Secure the foil more tightly over the top of the roast.

5. Roast the pork for 3 hours. Open up the foil and continue roasting until the meat is lightly browned, 30 minutes to 1 hour more. Baste occasionally with the pan juices. Let the pork rest for several minutes and then carve into ½-inch-thick slices. Nap with the pan juices and serve at once.

Makes 8 to 10 servings

# crispy duckling with Apricot Mirepoix And Mixed olives

I unabashedly adore many things about the French, but when it comes to the cooking of feathered friends, we often part company. For all the outrageous gastronomic seduction synonymous with French cuisine, I am continually surprised that these be-toqued Gauls often find pale and loose braised poultry skin preferable to irresistibly golden, crisp, and crackling roasted skin.

Throughout the Midi, recipes abound for both chicken and duck braised with olives. As much as I favor the notion of the savor gleaned from cooking with olives, I simply cannot stomach the thought of all that fat from the likes of one of our Long Island ducklings melting imperceptibly into a braising liquid. If I am indeed to celebrate the celebrated French paradox and its adjunct theory that duck fat has cholesterol-lowering qualities akin to olive oil, then I want to enjoy every morsel of duck fat consumed in the crispiest and most enticing form possible—impeccably well roasted skin!

157

*Et voilà!* Here is a recipe in which the ducks are butterflied by removing the backbones and then flattened and roasted until tender with very crisp skin. The backbones are then simmered along with the giblets and necks to make a tasty duck stock, which in turn serves as the base for a separately made sauce. This sauce begins with sautéing a classic vegetable *mirepoix* that is next enlivened with the sweet tang of dried apricots which balance the mildly bitter green and black olives. In short, a stupendous means of having a flavorful sauce and a crisp-skinned bird, too.

2 Long Island ducklings (4 to 5 pounds each)
Sea or coarse salt and freshly ground black pepper,
    to taste
1 tablespoon herbes de Provence
7 cups water
1 onion, quartered
2 carrots, broken into coarse chunks
2 ribs celery, broken into coarse chunks
Several sprigs fresh parsley

APRICOT AND OLIVE SAUCE
2 tablespoons duck fat or olive oil
1 medium onion, minced
¾ cup minced fennel bulb or celery
2 carrots, peeled and minced
2 cloves garlic, minced
10 dried apricot halves, cut into
    thin slivers

½ cup dry white wine
2 cups reduced duck stock (see step 2)
2 tablespoons honey
2 tablespoons fresh rosemary, coarsely chopped
½ cup imported green olives, blanched in boiling water for 1 minute
    and then drained
½ cup imported black olives, blanched in boiling water for 1 minute
    and then drained
Sea or coarse salt and freshly ground black pepper, to taste

1. Early in the day, prepare the ducks: Remove the giblets and necks from the duck cavities and set aside. Remove the backbones by cutting down the length of the ducks on both sides of the bone with a sharp knife or poultry shears. Reserve the

backbones. Lay the ducks out flat and press down on the breastbones with the palm of your hand to crack them and flatten the duck further. Sprinkle the ducks all over with salt, pepper, and the *herbes de Provence.* Arrange the ducks on a roasting pan and store them, uncovered, in the refrigerator or other cool place for 6 hours. The exposure to the air will help dry out the duck skin and make it more crisp when cooked.

2. Place the reserved giblets, necks, and backbones in a stockpot and cover them with the water. Add the onion, carrots, celery, and parsley sprigs to the pot. Bring the mixture to a boil and let it simmer, uncovered for 1½ to 2 hours. Strain the duck stock into a clean saucepan, discarding the solids. Reduce the stock over high heat to 2 cups, 20 to 30 minutes, and then set aside.

3. Preheat the oven to 425°F.

4. Remove the ducks from the refrigerator. Prick the skins all over with the tines of a fork. Roast the ducks for 30 minutes and then reduce the oven temperature to 325°F. Continue roasting the ducks until the skin is golden brown and crisp all over and the meat is very tender, about 1½ hours more.

5. While the ducks are roasting, make the sauce: Heat the duck fat or olive oil in a medium-size saucepan over medium-high heat. Add the onion, fennel, carrots, and garlic, and sauté until quite soft, about 10 minutes. Add the apricot slivers and sauté a few minutes more. Pour in the wine and reduced duck stock and let the sauce simmer, uncovered, for 15 minutes. Stir in the honey, rosemary, and blanched olives. Season the sauce with salt and pepper and keep warm over low heat until the ducks have finished roasting.

6. To serve the ducklings, split each one in half and place a half duckling in the center of each dinner plate. Spoon a generous amount of sauce over and around each duckling half. Serve at once. Any side dishes should be served on a separate plate.

*serves 4*

159

*AND WHAT ABOUT GARLIC* as a foundation of the cooking— as the essential element of so many dishes to which Provence is devoted—the aïoli, the garlic mayonnaise with the fish of the Friday lunch; the rouille, the version made with mashed potatoes and hot peppers; the brandade de morue, the pâté of cod, garlic, and olive oil; the aïgo bollido, one of the many soups made from garlic-scented water, of which another is the aïga saou, the "salted water" of Nice; and, of course, to cut an infinite list short, the pistou, the Provençal version of the pesto of Genoa. The list—and the jokes about garlic— could fill a book. It was Fred Allen who said that, in Provence, almost everyone should be arrested for fragrancy.

—ROY ANDRIES DE GROOT
*IN SEARCH OF THE PERFECT MEAL*

160

# Long-Simmered Chicken with Lots and Lots of garlic

I believe Julia Child was the first to popularize this fabulous Provençal chicken recipe during the seventies, when she hosted her *Cooking for Company* television series and wrote the *Julia Child & Company* cookbooks. At the time it was considered adventuresome, if not avant-garde, to use forty or more cloves of garlic in a single recipe. What a difference a couple of decades

have made, as now the appetizer of a whole roasted bulb of garlic served with goat cheese and toasted French bread has become
so commonplace as to be verging on cliché.

This garlic-rich chicken, however, is one dish I hope never
to see retired. When making the recipe, if I have on hand a batch
of garlic that peels easily, I prefer to do so, but many make the
dish more rustically with unpeeled garlic that is later squeezed
from its skin by each diner. My version further emphasizes the
natural sweetness of slowly roasted garlic by adding Provence's
pleasantly sweet Muscat de Beaumes-de-Venise wine as cooking
liquid. The Vaucluse village of Beaumes is as sweet as its wine,
and my bicycle always seems to exit the towered Romanesque
town happily burdened with a bottle or two of the namesake
amber wine.

2 chickens (3 to 3½ pounds each), quartered
¼ cup fruity olive oil
2 teaspoons dried tarragon
Sea or coarse salt and freshly ground black pepper, to taste
4 heads garlic, cloves separated and either peeled or not
1 bulb fennel, trimmed, cored, and cut into ⅓-inch-wide julienne
2½ cups Muscat de Beaumes-de-Venise, or other muscat
    dessert wine

1. Preheat the oven to 350°F.

2. Toss the chicken and oil together to coat the chicken and then arrange the pieces in a single layer in a large roasting pan. Sprinkle with the tarragon, salt, and pepper. Scatter the garlic cloves and fennel strips over and in between the chicken pieces. Pour the wine evenly over all.

3. Cover the pan tightly with aluminum foil and cook for 1 hour and 45 minutes. Uncover the pan, baste the chicken with the pan juices, and continue cooking until the skin becomes lightly browned on top, about 30 minutes more. Serve hot. Any leftovers are equally delicious reheated the following day.

makes 6 to 8 servings

162

# chicken with tomatoes, tarragon vinegar, and crème fraîche

eating in Gordes's tiny Comptoir du Victuailler restaurant is certain to bring gustatory rewards, like finding the perfect rendition of the classic French dish, chicken with tomatoes, tarragon, and vinegar. Being the lucky sole diner at the restaurant on a deserted Sunday evening in May brought me the added benefit of being treated to the gracious owner's undivided attention.

My evening began on a promising note with glasses of delicious red Rhône wine from the well-chosen wine list, and ended with my stomach sublimely sated and my notepad overflowing with a wealth of recipe tips from the passionately opinionated proprietor. A casual nibble on a few very smooth and meaty black olives paved the way for a breathtaking first course of perfectly peeled, warm, plump native asparagus, accompanied by a small bowl of Provence's best olive oil, seasoned with the faintest whisper of vinegar, salt, and cracked black pepper. All the zillions of other asparagus spears I had consumed in my life suddenly seemed like pale imitations of those that would not remain for very long in front of me.

Next followed a fragrant piece of tender chicken swimming in a silky sauce of fresh tomatoes, bright green tarragon, and pungent vinegar, whose acidity was mellowed by a secret balancing ingredient, which I suspected was butter. But the proprietor confessed to it being crème fraîche, while plying me with dessert—the Comptoir's acclaimed lavender-honey ice cream, insistently accompanied by a slice of sinful flourless chocolate cake. This winning combination of herby ice cream with dense bittersweet chocolate instantly cultivated in me a craving so strong, that I am glad that all my subsequent trips to Gordes have included a tor-tuous ascent by bicycle. This is not to say, however, that dupli-cating the Comptoir's marvelous chicken recipe shouldn't also be considered a feat and feather in my *panier*.

3 tablespoons olive oil
2 chickens (about 3 pounds each), cut into 6 to 8 serving pieces
    per chicken
Sea or coarse salt and freshly ground black pepper, to taste
1 large onion, minced
5 cloves garlic, minced
3 large carrots, peeled and cut into ¼-inch dice
2 heaping tablespoons tomato paste
1½ pounds ripe tomatoes, seeded and coarsely chopped
1 cup tarragon vinegar
1½ cups dry white wine
¼ cup coarsely chopped fresh tarragon, or 1½ tablespoons dried
1 teaspoon dried thyme
⅔ cup crème fraîche or heavy (or whipping) cream

1. Heat the olive oil in a heavy, large deep skillet or Dutch oven over medium-high heat. Season the chicken pieces with salt and pepper and add to the skillet, in batches if necessary, to brown all sides, 5 to 7 minutes per batch. Transfer the chicken to a platter.

2. Add the onion, garlic, and carrots to the skillet and sauté until softened, about 5 minutes. Stir in the tomato paste, tomatoes, vinegar, wine, tarragon, and thyme; bring to a simmer. Return the chicken pieces to the pot, cover, and simmer over medium heat until the chicken is quite tender, 45 minutes to 1 hour. Transfer the cooked chicken to a platter and keep warm.

3. Bring the sauce to a boil and cook until thickened and reduced by roughly one third, about 15 minutes. Stir in the crème fraîche or

heavy cream and continue to boil for 5 minutes more. Correct the seasoning with additional salt and pepper, if needed. Return the chicken pieces to the pot, nap with the sauce, and simmer just until heated through, 4 to 5 minutes. Serve the chicken hot with plenty of sauce spooned over it.

Makes 6 to 8 servings

## GORDES AFTER DARK

My first visit to the medieval hilltop village of Gordes, dubbed by *le tout Paris* as the sixteenth *arrondissement* of the Lubéron, fell on a sunny Sunday in late May, and its steep and narrow arched alleyways and main place de Château were swarming with people. So this is the town that epitomizes the low-key, wild, and tranquil allure of the Lubéron, I wondered to myself. I might well have left, had I not found a quaint rosemary-fringed room looking back across and up at the town's beautiful golden silhouette of terraced gardens and tiered stone houses, culminating in the round and turreted towers of the massive Renaissance château, now ironically home to the op-art Vasarely Museum.

My hotel was aptly named Les Romarins (the rosemarys), and I passed the late-afternoon hours reading while inhaling therapeutic wafts of piny rosemary and glancing in awe as the setting sun made my already incomparable panorama of this famed *village perché* all the more incredible.

Following a flowered path across a gully and then back up to the center of town, I returned at 8 P.M. to discover a dark and delightfully deserted Gordes. My nose took me into the tiny restaurant Comptoir du Victuailler, and I sat down to one of the most memorably simple meals I have ever eaten.

# Nito's poulet à la provençale

N ito is a vibrant and voluptuous Egyptian-born cook who, along with her American husband, David Carpita, runs the Mas de Cornud—a country inn devoted to the culinary arts and located in an eighteenth-century Provençal farmhouse on the outskirts of St.-Rémy. When not traveling, orchestrating gastronomic vacations, or overseeing guest chef cooking classes at the Mas, the Carpitas will host a home-cooked dinner for a lucky passing group of Butterfield & Robinson cyclists. These evenings begin outdoors under towering plane trees with David pouring *apéros* of *pastis* and Côteaux des Baux wines before retiring to the *bouledrome,* where he offers keen lessons on playing *pétanque,* the Provençal name for the beloved game of *boules.* Nito, meanwhile, reigns in the kitchen, sending forth baskets of dewy *crudités* from her garden and putting the finishing touches on the evening's meal.

While Nito's specialty is Middle Eastern cooking, she knows how to add her own delicious spin to Provençal fare, and those evenings passed clustered around the grand banquet table set in the center of the Mas de Cornud's kitchen are always warmly remembered. The courses are served family style from steaming terra-cotta platters placed in rows down the center of the table. Rustic dishes such as tender stewed rabbit, or this saucy, olive-speckled, Provençal-style *poulet,* or chicken, are usually featured and accompanied by nutty mounds of the region's unique Risotto d'Epeautre (see Index). Ever-flowing local wines tend to encourage group-embellished boasts of biking over the increasingly steep, crenelated peaks of the Alpilles mountains. Desserts such as float-ing islands finally send all but insomniac guides and cooks float-ing back to our hotel for another hard-earned night of sound sleep. Some recipes, after all, are best gleaned over a nightcap.

¼ pound salt pork, cut into ¼-inch dice
2 chickens (2½ to 3 pounds each), quartered
Sea or coarse salt and freshly ground black pepper, to taste
⅓ cup whiskey
½ cup dry white wine
1 can (28 ounces) diced tomatoes
3 tablespoons tomato paste
2 tablespoons fresh thyme or
    ½ teaspoon dried
3 bay leaves
1 tablespoon olive oil
2 large cloves garlic, minced
1 cup Niçois olives, unpitted

167

1. Sauté the salt pork in a large, heavy, deep skillet or Dutch oven over medium-high heat until just beginning to brown, 5 to 6 minutes. Remove with a slotted spatula to drain on paper towels. Season the chicken pieces with salt and pepper and brown on all sides in the fat remaining in the skillet, in batches if necessary, 5 to 7 minutes per batch. Remove from the heat. Return all the chicken pieces to the skillet. Pour the whiskey into the skillet and standing back, carefully light it with a long kitchen match to flambé the chicken. When the flames subside, transfer the chicken to a platter.

2. Add the wine, tomatoes, tomato paste, thyme, and bay leaves to the skillet. Bring to a simmer over medium-high heat. Return the chicken and salt pork to the pot, cover, and simmer over medium heat until the chicken is very tender, 45 minutes to 1 hour.

3. If the sauce seems too thin, remove the chicken pieces and keep warm while boiling the sauce to reduce and thicken it to the desired consistency. This is usually accomplished within 12 to 15 minutes. Return the chicken to the pot.

4. Just before serving, heat the olive oil in a small skillet over medium-high heat. Add the garlic and olives and sauté until warmed through, 2 to 3 minutes. Stir into the sauce with the chicken and serve the chicken at once with plenty of sauce spooned over it. Be sure to warn your guests that the tiny and delicious Niçois olives are not pitted.

makes 6 to 8 servings

THE BLACK TRUFFLES OF VAUCLUSE, either wild from the heavily guarded allotments on Mont Ventoux or from plantations like Dijour's, ripen only after the first frost, and it's then the fun or fuming begins. Tell it not in Périgord, but Provence now secretly supplements that overreputed region's truffle production—as anyone prepared to brave the Carpentras truffle market at 8 a.m. on a cold February morning can, at risk of life and limb, discover.

—JULIAN MORE
A TASTE OF PROVENCE

# pAʃtiʃ-ʃouʃed rabbit

‿◡

t o me, *pastis*-soused rabbit is the quintessential Provençal main dish. The rabbit is typically French, while its sauce of simmered *pastis*, tomatoes, garlic, olives, and basil is oh so Provençal. Even if you do not view *pastis*, as "the milk of Provence," as writer Peter Mayle does, you should still try this dish as a means of introducing *pastis* into your diet in a less lethal form than the norm of a cloudy yellow, anise-intense apéritif consumed with abandon in cafés south of Valence. If it's the thought of rabbit that's making you stove-shy, then feel free to substitute a cut-up chicken for the rabbit in the recipe.

169

1 rabbit (about 3 pounds), cut into 6 to 8 serving pieces
½ cup pastis, such as Pernod or Ricard
¼ cup plus 2 tablespoons olive oil
Freshly ground black pepper, to taste
2 medium onions, cut into crescent-shaped slivers
4 large ripe tomatoes, seeded and diced
6 cloves garlic, minced
1½ teaspoons fennel seeds
⅔ cup imported black olives, pitted and coarsely chopped
1 bunch fresh basil, leaves slivered
Sea or coarse salt, to taste
Cooked fettuccine or wide egg noodles, for serving

1. The day before you plan to serve the rabbit, arrange the pieces in a single layer in a shallow glass dish. Drizzle them with the *pastis*

and ¼ cup of the olive oil. Season generously with the pepper. Cover the dish with plastic wrap and let marinate overnight in the refrigerator.

2. The following day, heat the remaining 2 tablespoons olive oil in a Dutch oven over medium heat. Add the onions and sauté until softened, 5 to 7 minutes. Add the tomatoes, garlic, and fennel seeds and continue cooking, stirring frequently, until the mixture begins to become saucelike, 12 to 15 minutes.

3. Add the rabbit along with its marinade to the pot, covering the pieces by spooning the vegetables over the top of them. Cover the pot and let all simmer together over medium-low heat for 30 minutes. Add the olives and half the slivered basil to the pot, reserving the rest for garnishing. Cover the pot and continue simmering, stirring occasionally, until the rabbit is tender, 20 to 30 minutes more. Season to taste with salt.

4. Serve the rabbit with plenty of its sauce, atop a bed of cooked fettuccine or noodles. Garnish each serving generously with the remaining slivered basil. Serve at once.

Makes 4 servings

# MARKET DAY

## INSPIRATIONS

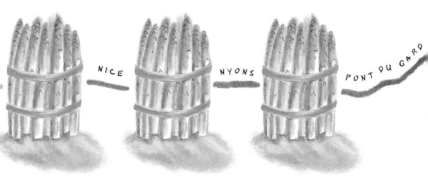

MONT VENTOUX    NICE    NYONS    PONT DU GARD

..................................................

*THE BEST WAY* to strike up an acquaintance with one of these Provençal towns is to arrive around daybreak, preferably on a market day when the place is full of sleepy vendors unloading their vans and trucks of everything you can imagine from pigeons and hams to olives and plums. The whole town seems to be stretching and yawning and waiting for the sunrise to warm it up.

—LAWRENCE DURRELL
*CAESAR'S VAST GHOST—ASPECTS OF PROVENCE*

..................................................

Happening upon a village, large or small, perched or tucked away, on its designated market day is one of the most fascinating and potentially broadening experiences when bicycling through Provence. The biggest markets, like those in Arles, L'Isle-sur-la-Sorgue, and Vaison-la-Romaine, snake across vast nooks and crannies of the town and offer everything from *aubergines,* antiques, and olives to sachets of lavender, spit-roasted rabbits, enviable tomatoes, and wildflower honey. It's easy to while away the morning hours putting together a portable picnic to highlight midday on the cycling route. Aromatic and crispy-skinned roast chickens, piquant goat cheeses, glistening green *olives cassées,* yeasty *fougasses,* and seasonal fresh fruits—strawberries, cherries, Cavaillon melons, or figs—are all favorite edibles with my pedaling groups.

Stopping in these lively markets can also be one of the more frustrating experiences for a cook like myself, who has ready access to a bicycle but not a kitchen burner. When I host *aïoli* picnics *sur l'herbe* for my groups, I have a field day loading up at the nearest village's outdoor market on every conceivable vegetable that can be dipped raw into my garlicky mortar. But since I honestly yearn to cook each and every piece of gorgeous Provençal produce in sight and lose myself in the sublime repertoire of regional vegetable recipes, I commit my visits to sensory memory and unleash their myriad inspirations with a fury once I'm back in my home kitchen. In this way, the soul of Provençal cuisine remains near and dear to my heart, whether stateside, stoveside, or beside myself with longing for a kitchen to call my own when pedaling through the bountiful South of France.

# Artichokes
# à la barigoule

These braised artichokes are a Provençal classic, though every time I order them in a regional restaurant, they seem to be prepared differently. In fact, there's even local disagreement over how the dish received its name. Some believe the name derives

from a time-honored method of cooking artichokes with a mush-room known as *barigoulo* in old Provençal dialect. Others believe the dish was named because the artichokes were cooked or grilled in the same manner as mushrooms, and still others say that *barigoule* "stems" from the fact that whole, upside-down artichokes bear poetic resemblance to mushrooms.

174

Since I find all these explanations plausible, I decided it would be equally logical to blend the best of all *les artichauts à la barigoule* recipes I've tasted into my own rendition. Often times, the brais-ing companions of the artichokes are strained out so that the cooked artichokes swim in a classy clear broth, but I personally prefer the more colorful and rustic look of leaving carrots, onions, garlic, and prosciutto slivers wedged in every conceivable nook and cranny of the artichokes. Additionally, my recipe here is adapted to globe artichokes, since never in North America have I come across the delightfully chokeless violet artichokes that grow in Provence.

All said and done, Artichokes à la Barigoule make an ideal year-round first course or light luncheon on a sultry summer day.

1 lemon

4 large globe artichokes

¼ cup fruity olive oil

1 large onion, peeled and cut into thin rings

2 large carrots, peeled and cut into ½-inch-thick
    rounds

3 ounces thinly sliced prosciutto, coarsely shredded

¼ pound white mushrooms, thinly sliced

1 cup dry white wine

8 sun-dried tomato halves (the redder the better),
    cut into thin slivers

3 large cloves garlic, coarsely chopped

Sea or coarse salt and freshly ground black pepper,
    to taste

⅓ cup minced fresh parsley or slivered basil
    for garnish

¼ cup coarsely grated Parmesan cheese (optional)

175

1. Fill a large bowl with cold water. Halve and juice the lemon, adding both the juice and the squeezed lemon to the bowl of water. Trim the stem of each artichoke to measure about 1 inch from the base. Slice 1 inch off the top of each artichoke. Snap off the tough lower leaves by bending them back to their natural breaking points. Using scissors, trim off the prickly points of the remaining visible leaves. Halve the artichokes vertically and scrape away the hairy chokes with a small spoon or paring knife. Cut each artichoke half vertically again into 3 wedges and dunk them immediately into the bowl of lemon water. Set aside.

2. Heat the olive oil over medium-high heat in a large, wide pot. Add the onion and carrots and sauté until softened, about 5 minutes. Add the prosciutto and mushrooms and continue sautéing until the mushrooms are softened, 3 minutes more. Drain the artichoke

wedges, reserving 2 cups of the lemon water. Add the wedges to the pot, stirring to coat them well with the vegetables and oil. Add the wine and sun-dried tomatoes, bring the liquid to a boil, and let it reduce by half, 5 to 7 minutes.

3. Scatter the garlic around the artichokes and pour in the reserved 2 cups of lemon water. Season with salt and pepper, cover the pot, and simmer over medium-low heat until the artichokes are tender, 25 to 30 minutes. Transfer all to a shallow platter or serving dish. Garnish with either parsley or basil and a sprinkling of Parmesan, if desired.

Makes 4 to 6 servings

176

# ultimate Asparagus

Scheduling on the home front had for years dictated that I confine my bicycle guiding services to the autumn of each year. When freedom to travel to Europe in the spring breezed my way, I seized the opportunity to head directly to Provence. What a thrill it was to see this beloved pocket of France ablaze in shades of spring green, purple iris, and bright yellow Scotch broom, rather than parched by a relentless summer sun into autumnal earth tones. But the grandest thrill of all was having occasion to savor at long last the legendary asparagus of the region. Any amount of descriptive hyperbole applied to the platter of warm, perfectly peeled and cooked spears set before me on that memorable May evening when I first dined in the tiny Comptoir du

Victuailler in Gordes could only be an understatement. In short, asparagus sown in the warm and rich soil of Provence is one of the world's great gastronomic treasures. The only embellishment befitting such perfection is a drizzle of the region's most esteemed olive oil, from the old mill in Maussane-les-Alpilles, adulterated by the merest hint of fine white-wine or Champagne vinegar.

Back home, I celebrate the spirit, if not the incomparable flavor, of Provence's asparagus by serving in season the best and most freshly picked local asparagus, peeled impeccably, cooked crisply, and drizzled with the finest extra-virgin olive oil in my pantry—perhaps one carried home from the mill in Maussane if I'm lucky.

> 2 pounds freshly picked asparagus, trimmed and
>     carefully peeled
> ½ cup top-quality extra-virgin olive oil
> Whisper of white wine vinegar or Champagne
>     vinegar
> Sea or coarse salt and freshly ground black pepper,
>     to taste

177

1. Lay the asparagus spears in a wide, shallow pot and pour in enough water so that it covers the asparagus by 1 inch. Bring to a boil over high heat and cook until the asparagus is just crisp-tender, 3 to 5 minutes, depending on the thickness of the spears. Drain thoroughly.

2. While the asparagus is cooking, whisk the olive oil with the vinegar in a small serving dish. Arrange the warm asparagus on serving plates and let each person drizzle his or her own asparagus with the olive oil mixture and season with the salt and pepper. Eat slowly, spear by spear, reflecting upon its opulent simplicity.

Makes 4 to 6 servings

# Avocado, olive, and orange salad with pastis

I came across the idea for this unique salad in an article in a French magazine on *"pastis dans la cuisine."* The article began: "Forget sipping *pastis* as an *apéritif* under Provençal plane trees, for with its essence of the Midi, *pastis* brings to the plate all the warmth, richness, and perfumes of this region where the cicadas sing." After such poetic enticement, I naturally couldn't resist toting my bottle of *pastis* from the bar into the kitchen, where it did quite sufficiently succeed in bringing the delectable tastes and memories of my Provençal meanderings to the salad plate. The pretty presentation of fanned pale green avocado slices alternating with bright, *pastis*-infused oranges cools on the sultriest of summer evenings, but also can add a touch of yearned-for sunshine to the winter table.

4 oranges, peel, pith, and any seeds removed,
    thinly sliced
⅓ cup pastis, such as Pernod or Ricard
⅓ cup fruity olive oil
¼ cup fresh lime juice
2 to 3 drops hot sauce, such as Tabasco
Sea or coarse salt, to taste
2 ripe avocados, preferably Hass
⅓ cup imported black olives, pitted and coarsely
    chopped

1. Toss the oranges and *pastis* together and let marinate in the refrigerator for at least 30 minutes but no longer than 3 hours.

2. Whisk together the olive oil, lime juice, and hot sauce. Season with salt.

3. To assemble individual salads: Cut the avocados in half lengthwise and remove the pits and the skin. Slice each avocado half lengthwise into thin slices and fan the slices from each half onto 1 of 4 salad plates. Drizzle the olive oil-lime vinaigrette over the slices. Insert the chilled and macerated slices from 1 orange in between the avocado slices on each plate. Top each salad with a sprinkling of the olives. Serve at once.

makes 4 servings

179

# cAuliflower
# À LA grecque

Vegetables *à la grecque* was one of the first dishes I learned to make when I cooked part-time during my college years in a few cutting-edge Cambridge, Massachusetts, restaurants. Since then, I often forget how delicious and sophisticated vegetables afloat in the coriander-spiked liquid characteristic of the *à la grecque* preparation can be. But I was recently agreeably reminded when this refreshing cauliflower *à la grecque* appeased a hungry edge after an invigorating day's cycle. It was served as part of a complimentary appetizer plate in the stone-vaulted dining room of the splendid Hostellerie de Crillon-le-Brave. Here is chef Philippe Monti's recipe.

> 1½ *cups dry white wine*
> 1 *teaspoon sugar*
> 2 *strips lemon peel, 1 inch wide*
> ¼ *cup fresh lemon juice*
> 2 *tablespoons whole coriander seeds, coarsely cracked in a mortar and pestle or spice grinder*
> 2 *bay leaves*
> 1 *medium head cauliflower, cored and trimmed into 1- to 2-inch florets*
> *Sea or coarse salt and freshly ground black pepper, to taste*
> *Extra-virgin olive oil, for serving*

1. Combine the wine, sugar, lemon peel, lemon juice, coriander, and bay leaves in a large, nonreactive saucepan. Bring to a simmer over medium heat and cook for 5 minutes. Add the cauliflower florets and continue simmering, stirring occasionally, until the florets are crisp-tender, 10 to 12 minutes. Let the cauliflower cool in the cooking liquid. Season with salt and pepper, transfer to a dish, and chill in the refrigerator until ready to serve.

2. To serve the cauliflower, spoon a few florets with a little of their liquid onto a small plate. Drizzle with a little olive oil and enjoy. Cauliflower *à la grecque* will keep in the refrigerator for up to 1 week.

Makes 12 to 15 appetizer servings

# baſil-ſtrewn ſtring bean ſalad

$\backsim$

$\int$imone Beck, or Simca, was best known in America as the French woman who collaborated with Julia Child on the two classic cooking tomes devoted to *Mastering the Art of French Cooking*. She also wrote two books on her own (*Simca's Cuisine* and *New Menus From Simca's Cuisine*), and both were extremely inspirational for me during my early and formative years in the kitchen. Since much of Simca's cooking style reflected the period of time she spent living in the South of France, I naturally relished a return to her books during the process of researching Provençal cuisine for this book.

181

Simca's imaginative menu combinations and recipes once again managed to give me another whole level of appreciation. This stunning and delicious green bean salad, inspired by Simca's *Salade de Haricots Verts, Provençale* is but one example of how her work continues to expand my culinary palate. Indeed, the rich flavors and colors of the salad can make me altogether forget my usual aversion to the fatter and tougher variety of string beans prevalent in North America. The salad's basil vinaigrette will taste best if made in a mortar and pestle, though a food processor may be employed if I haven't yet managed to make you a convert to the mortar and pestle.

BASIL VINAIGRETTE
3 cloves garlic, peeled
½ teaspoon sea or coarse salt
1 cup loosely packed fresh basil
3 tablespoons fresh lemon juice
½ cup olive oil

BEAN SALAD
1 pound green beans, trimmed and sliced in half
      lengthwise
4 large ripe plum tomatoes, seeded and diced
1 cup imported black olives, pitted and coarsely
      chopped
6 anchovy fillets, drained and finely minced
1 bulb fennel, trimmed, cored, and thinly sliced
½ cup slivered fresh basil
Sea or coarse salt and freshly ground black pepper,
      to taste
3 large hard-cooked eggs, peeled and chopped

1. To make the basil vinaigrette: Mash the garlic and salt together in a mortar and pestle to form a paste. Add a few basil leaves at a time and continue mashing into a paste until all of the leaves have been incorporated. Slowly blend in the lemon juice and olive oil. Let stand while making the salad. Alternatively, the garlic, salt, and basil may be minced together in a food processor and then the lemon juice and oil added through the feed tube while the machine is running.

2. To make the salad: Bring a large pot of salted water to a boil,

add the beans, and cook until just crisp-tender, 2 to 3 minutes. Drain and refresh under cold running water. Drain again.

3. In a large mixing bowl, combine the tomatoes, olives, and anchovies. Stir in the beans and fennel. Add the basil vinaigrette and toss all together to coat thoroughly. Stir in the shredded basil and season the salad with salt and pepper. Chill the salad for a few hours to mellow the flavors. Just before serving, stir in the chopped eggs. Serve cold or at room temperature.

Makes 6 to 8 servings

# chopped salade Niçoise

A s of late, there seems to be a lot of revamping of the clas-sic *salade niçoise,* with the most frequent alteration coming from trendsetting chefs who substitute seared rare fresh tuna for the canned tuna in the original recipe. My version tends to fall somewhere in between. Rather than artistically composing the many ingredients of the salad, I chop and toss them all together in the manner of those dated chopped salads that are suddenly resurfacing on menus of many a hot new restaurant. As a rule, however, I side with canned tuna classicists, though if there hap-pened to be a leftover grilled tuna steak lurking in my refrigera-tor, I wouldn't hesitate to flake it into my *niçoise.*

The skinny little French string beans, known as *haricots verts,* are the best bean for a *salade niçoise,* but if they are difficult to find, choose the youngest and tenderest green beans available. Finally, I've buried the requisite anchovies in a paste that's whisked into my salad vinaigrette.

VINAIGRETTE
1 tablespoon anchovy paste
1 tablespoon imported Dijon mustard
2 tablespoons fresh lemon juice
1 large clove garlic, minced
1 tablespoon grated lemon zest
1 teaspoon sea or coarse salt
½ cup fruity olive oil

SALAD
3 large potatoes, peeled and cut into ½-inch cubes
½ pound tender, young green beans, trimmed and cut into
    2-inch lengths
¼ cup dry white wine
1 roasted red bell pepper (page 135), diced,
    or 1 cup minced jarred pimiento
1 bunch scallions, trimmed and minced
2 tablespoons drained capers
⅔ cup pitted and coarsely chopped imported black olives
1 can (13 ounces) water-packed tuna, drained and flaked
3 medium tomatoes, seeded and diced
5 large hard-cooked eggs, peeled and minced
⅓ cup pine nuts, lightly toasted
Sea or coarse salt and freshly ground black pepper,
    to taste
1 head romaine lettuce, dark outer leaves removed
    and saved for another use
½ cup shredded fresh basil

1. To make the vinaigrette, whisk together the anchovy paste, mustard, and lemon juice in a small bowl. Add the garlic, lemon zest, and salt. Slowly whisk in the olive oil. Set aside.

2. To make the salad, place the potatoes in a large pot and cover with water. Bring to a boil and continue cooking until the potatoes are tender but not mushy, 12 to 15 minutes. Meanwhile, bring another pot of water to a boil and blanch the beans until crisp-tender, 2 to 3 minutes. Drain both the potatoes and beans. Place them in a large bowl and immediately toss them with the white wine and about half the vinaigrette. Stir in the roasted pepper, scallions, capers, olives, and tuna. The salad may be made up to this point and held at room temperature for 2 hours before proceeding with the rest of the recipe, if desired.

3. As close to serving time as possible, mix the tomatoes, eggs, and pine nuts into the salad. Moisten with a little more vinaigrette and season with salt and pepper. Shred the romaine lettuce into ¾-inch-wide strips and toss with the basil and the remaining vinaigrette. Make a bed of the lettuce mixture over the bottom of a large serving platter. Top with the chopped *niçoise* mixture and serve at once.

Makes 6 main course salad servings

# MESCLUN

I remember spying a mesclun salad for the first time on a menu in Paris back in the mid-1980s. Since it was unknown to me, I asked my French hosts what mesclun was. They explained that it was a mix of many different baby salad greens harvested in Provence in the dewy hours of the early morning. Of course I ordered the salad, and it was love at first multicolored, delicate, feathery, and peppery bite. Never did I imagine that a decade later mesclun would become all the rage in North America and be sold in supermarkets nationwide. Americans tend to like the convenience, if not the priciness, of being able to buy a beautiful array of already mixed and cleaned greens to toss into salads of all sorts.

In Provence, however, the mix of baby greens—red and green oak leaf lettuce, mâche, frisée, arugula, and nasturtium flowers, to name a few—is served solo, dressed with only fine olive oil, salt, and pepper—no vinegar, lemon juice, or mustard. Such minimalism allows all the various nuances of these tender greens to be savored to the fullest. Try making a mesclun salad in this simple way at home sometime, and I guarantee you'll want to continue tossing forever after in the true Provençal tradition.

# endive ribbons with creamy anchovy vinaigrette

～

$\int$ ome of the prettiest biking in Provence is to be found in the less touristed areas of northern Provence stretching around the Dentelles de Montmirail through the little wine villages of Beaumes-de-Venise and Vacqueyras, on up to the Roman town of Vaison-la-Romaine, and beyond to the protected olive groves of Nyons and the vibrant lavender fields of Grignan. I reveled in this getaway not long ago and discovered this unusual endive salad on the menu at lunch on the second day of the trip.

I had passed a leisurely morning cycling with a friend in the flat plains sprawling beneath the shadows of the distant, towering Mont Ventoux and jagged Dentelles de Montmirail. *Dentelle* means lace in French and aptly describes these doilylike, mountainous limestone formations. We stopped often to check out colorful, small-scale flower and food markets in sleepy, one-fountain villages en route before meeting up with the rest of our group for a pre-lunch wine tasting at the beautiful, state-of-the-art Château Pesquié. Now, I'm not sure whether it was the daintiness of the lacy Dentelles or my slight light-headedness from sipping the wine, but I found myself subliminally craving something equally light and dainty come lunch hour at a neighboring restaurant. This refreshing and simple salad of shredded ribbons of pale green endive tossed in a just-sharp-enough creamy anchovy vinaigrette certainly hit the spot. When

187

not served solo as a light luncheon, the salad makes a smart pre- or post-dinner offering.

1 shallot, minced
1 large clove garlic, minced
8 anchovy fillets, drained
1½ tablespoons imported Dijon mustard
1 large egg yolk (see Box, facing page)
3 tablespoons fresh lemon juice
¾ cup fruity olive oil
8 heads Belgian endive, outer leaves discarded sliced horizontally into ½-inch-wide strips
Freshly ground black pepper, to taste

1. Place the shallot, garlic, and anchovies in a food processor; process to form a paste. Add the mustard, egg yolk, and lemon juice and pulse the machine to incorporate. With the machine running, pour the oil through the feed tube in a thin, steady stream to make a mayonnaise-like emulsion. Transfer the vinaigrette to a small bowl and store in the refrigerator until ready to use.

2. To make the salad, place the sliced endive in a large salad bowl. Toss with enough of the anchovy vinaigrette to coat the greens lightly all over. Season generously with black pepper and serve at once. Extra vinaigrette will keep in the refrigerator for up to 1 week and may be used to dress more endive salads or as a dip for raw vegetables.

Makes 4 to 6 servings

# THE RAW EGG QUESTION

Many of Provence's most renowned sauces—*aïoli, rouille, anchoïade*—are made with raw egg yolks and I must honestly say I've never heard one garlicky word uttered in Provence about the risk of coming down with food poisoning from the salmonella bacteria that can be harbored in uncooked eggs. I suspect the local wisdom conspires to have all convinced that the pungency of the ingredients in these lusty sauces is capable of overpowering anything potentially harmful. However, the fear of salmonella contamination is so great in the United States these days that magazines and newspapers will no longer print recipes that call for uncooked eggs. So, what are cooks with a passion for authentically made Provençal sauces to do?

I personally continue to use raw eggs in my own home, but I make sure that my eggs are as fresh as possible, come from a trusted local source, and are kept chilled in the coldest part of my refrigerator. If you don't, for whatever reason, have confidence in your own fresh egg source, then I recommend two acknowledged safe alternatives to using raw eggs in the recipes that call for them in this collection. The first option is to look for pasteurized eggs or egg substitutes in the dairy section of your supermarket and to substitute them for the raw eggs following the carton's instructions and guidelines.

A second option is to substitute a commercial, store-bought mayonnaise to replace the egg and oil emulsions that form the base of the Provençal sauces in this book. The mayonnaise should then be flavored accordingly with garlic, anchovies, lemon, saffron, or whatever seasonings a particular sauce calls for.

Individuals with additional questions about raw egg use may call the USDA Meat and Poultry Hotline: (800) 535-4555.

# joie d'endive

W hile the mild bitterness of cooked Belgian endive may be an acquired taste for some, it is one I adore. Elegant whole bulbs of endive are first browned in a little butter and then braised in a sweet bath of homemade *vin d'orange* flecked with salty pink slivers of prosciutto. A swirl of cream adds a final balancing enrichment that makes this vegetable dish truly fill me with *joie de vivre* every time I pair it with my recipe for Crispy Duckling with Apricot Mirepoix and Mixed Olives (page 156).

If you have been remiss in making your own private stash of *vin d'orange*, a store-bought bottle of the French apéritif Lillet enriched with a tablespoon or two of granulated sugar may be substituted.

190

> 1½ tablespoons unsalted butter
> 6 Belgian endives, blemished outer leaves removed
> 2 ounces thinly sliced prosciutto, cut into matchstick
>     slivers
> ½ cup Vin d'Orange (page 33)
> ⅓ cup heavy (or whipping) cream
> Sea or coarse salt and freshly ground black pepper,
>     to taste

1. Melt the butter over medium heat in a sauté pan just large enough to hold the endive in a single layer. Add the endives and sauté them, turning frequently, until lightly browned on all sides, 7 to 10 minutes.

2. Scatter the prosciutto slivers evenly over and in between the endives. Moisten all with the *Vin d'Orange*. Cover the pan and

braise the endives over low heat, turning them from time to time, until tender, about 45 minutes.

3. Uncover the pot, drizzle the cream over all, and then raise the heat so that the liquid comes to a boil. Shake the pan gently from time to time and cook until the liquid thickens slightly, 4 to 5 minutes. Season the endives with salt and pepper and serve at once.

Makeſ 4 to 6 ſervingſ

# braiſed feNNeL

In Provence, where the drinking of anise-scented *pastis* is regarded as a highly reputable pastime, the vegetable from which that potent apéritif is derived also enjoys great favor at the table. As a lover of fennel myself, I enthusiastically recommend everyone try this exceptionally sweet and mellow way of cooking pale green fennel bulbs at least once. Indeed, it is the surest way I know of becoming an instant fennel fan, and the recipe pairs magically as a vegetable accompaniment to many of the fish, poultry, and lamb dishes in the Provençal culinary repertoire.

> 3 medium fennel bulbs
> 1 tablespoon unsalted butter
> 1½ tablespoons olive oil
> 1½ teaspoons sugar
> ½ cup fresh orange juice
> ½ cup dry white wine
> 2 cloves garlic, peeled and cut into
>     thin slivers
> Sea or coarse salt and freshly ground
>     black pepper, to taste

192

1. Trim the long stalks and their feathery leaves from the fennel bulbs. Reserve a few of the leaves for garnishing. (The stalks may be saved for flavoring stocks, if desired.) Cut the bulbs in half lengthwise.

2. Heat the butter and oil together in a heavy skillet over medium-high heat. Sprinkle the sugar evenly over the bottom of the pan and then add the fennel, positioning it with cut sides down. Sauté until the undersides are well browned, 7 to 10 minutes.

3. Pour the orange juice and wine into the skillet. Scatter the slivered garlic in and around the fennel bulbs. Cover the pan, lower the heat to a simmer, and continue cooking until the fennel is quite soft, about 30 minutes. Season the fennel with salt and pepper, and garnish by mincing a couple tablespoons of the reserved fennel leaves and sprinkling them on top. Serve half a bulb per person with some of the pan juices spooned over and around the bulb.

Makes 6 servings

# sweet pepper gratin

the gutsy flavors of roasted sweet peppers, anchovies, olives, garlic, and goat cheese explode brilliantly when confined together in one intense little casserole. I'll often vary the color of the peppers I select for the gratin according to my artistic influence of the moment. If I happen to be thinking about Van Gogh and his giant sunflowers, I'll no doubt be prone to making a gratin of all yellow peppers. If my mood swings toward the vibrant mixed colors of Cézanne or Matisse, then a fiery mix of red and yellow peppers will suit just fine. Whatever the composition, the gratin may be served alone as a first course in the manner of a vegetable antipasto or as a splashy vegetable accompaniment to roasted or grilled meats or chicken.

193

6 red and/or yellow roasted bell peppers, in any color
    combination (see Box, page 135)
2½ tablespoons olive oil
6 anchovies, drained and minced
½ cup imported black olives, pitted and coarsely chopped
Freshly ground black pepper, to taste

TOPPING
1 cup fresh French bread crumbs
2 cloves garlic, chopped
½ cup minced fresh parsley
3 ounces creamy white goat cheese, crumbled
2 to 3 tablespoons olive oil

1. Preheat the oven to 350°F.

2. Cut the bell peppers lengthwise into strips ¾ inch wide. Toss the strips with the olive oil, anchovies, olives, and black pepper. Transfer to a shallow, 1-quart gratin dish.

3. Make the topping: Place the bread crumbs, garlic, and parsley together in a food processor and process until well combined. Add the goat cheese and pulse the machine to just barely incorporate the cheese. Crumble this mixture evenly over the peppers. Drizzle the top with olive oil to moisten.

4. Bake the gratin until the top is browned and crisp, 30 to 40 minutes. Serve hot, warm, or at room temperature.

Makes 4 to 6 servings

194

# crispy sautéed potatoes à la provençale

Now that I've mastered the technique of cooking these wonderfully simple and addictive potatoes, I find myself making them all the time. For sautéed potatoes to have a crispness nearly akin to that achieved by deep fat-frying, the peeled and cubed potatoes must be soaked and rinsed in cold water to remove the starch. If the potato's natural starch isn't removed, the cubes will stick to the pan and break down and become mushy during cooking—much like breakfast hash browns. With the starch removed, the potato cubes retain their shape and absorb very little of the cooking oil. Mustering up the patience to resist stirring and flipping the potatoes prematurely will yield irresistibly crunchy brown morsels. The caramelized garlic also adds to the recipe's sensual appeal. If tiny new potatoes are in season, by all means use them in this recipe, as they can be sautéed whole, thereby eliminating the peeling and soaking steps.

> 2½ pounds all-purpose potatoes, peeled and cut into 1-inch
>     cubes, or small (1 to 1½ inches in diameter) new
>     potatoes, unpeeled but scrubbed
> 3 tablespoons olive oil
> 20 to 24 cloves garlic, unpeeled
> ¼ cup minced fresh rosemary
> Sea or coarse salt and freshly ground black pepper, to taste

1. If using the all-purpose potatoes, place the cubes in a bowl and cover with cold water. Let soak for 15 minutes. Drain in a colander and then rinse under cold running water for an additional 5 minutes. Dry thoroughly with a kitchen towel. If using whole new potatoes, simply make sure they are well-dried after scrubbing.

2. Heat the olive oil in a very large skillet over medium-high heat. Add the potatoes and garlic, making sure that all fit in a single layer. If the potatoes are crowded into more than one layer, they will steam rather than crisp; use two skillets or work in batches if you do not have a large enough skillet. Let the potatoes brown on each side undisturbed for 5 to 7 minutes before flipping with a spatula to brown the other sides. Continue sautéing until the potatoes are browned and crisp all over, 20 to 25 minutes. Sprinkle with the rosemary and season with salt and pepper. Serve hot. If the potatoes are made in advance they may be held or reheated by placing them in a large baking pan in a 275°F oven until hot.

Makes 6 to 8 servings

# olive-smashed potatoes

**t**hese are the sort of mashed potatoes that can easily be consumed with abandon and therefore harbor the potential to induce penitent cycling ascents to the harsh, white limestone peak of Mont Ventoux (whose name more than coincidentally bears close resemblance to the French word for windy—*venteux*)! The winning recipe for them was inspired by Provençal chef Roger Vergé in his cookbook, *Les Legumes de Mon Moulin*.

Once the potatoes are cooked, they are not passed through a food mill to render them super silky, as required in the most sophisticated French recipes for puréed potatoes, but rather roughly smashed with a big balloon whisk or standard potato masher. This gives them a texture that to me personally and poetically recalls the rustic appeal of the gnarled olive trees that frequently grace the rugged Provençal landscape. The smashed potatoes are then sensuously enriched with warmed, golden-green, extra-virgin olive oil and flecked generously with coarsely chopped black Provençal olives.

I like to use Yukon Gold potatoes in this recipe to aid in making the color of the finished potatoes almost as richly golden in hue as the olive oil within. Olive-Smashed Potatoes are best consumed just after being made—not a difficult task!

*2 pounds Yukon Gold potatoes*
*⅓ to ½ cup extra-virgin olive oil, warmed in a saucepan*
  *over low heat*
*⅔ cup imported black olives, pitted and coarsely chopped*
*Sea or coarse salt and freshly ground black pepper, to taste*

1. Steam the potatoes in a vegetable steamer set over simmering water in a covered pot until tender, 25 to 30 minutes. Wearing rubber kitchen gloves to prevent burning your hands, peel the potatoes immediately.

2. Place the hot potatoes in a medium-size mixing bowl and coarsely mash them by gently pounding with a balloon whisk or potato masher. Gradually incorporate as much of the warmed olive oil as conscience allows. Gently fold in the olives and season to taste with salt and pepper. Indulge at once.

Makes 4 to 6 servings

197

# risotto d'épeautre

*épeautre*, as mentioned in the recipe for Soupe d'Epeautre, is an ancient Provençal strain of wheat grown primarily east of Mont Ventoux. It is much in vogue these days in Provence, prepared in a "risotto" fashion. Nito Carpita serves it with her

Poulet à la Provençale (see Index) at the Mas de Cornud, and I like it with just about anything and everything. I heartily encourage travelers to Provence to bring home some *épeautre* to make this addictive risotto, for when wheat berries are substituted in this particular recipe, the cooking time must be at least doubled and they will not absorb the broth in the same fashion as the *épeautre.* Fortunately, the end result will be as nutty and chewy as *épeautre,* and I realize that wheat berries may have to suffice as the only ticket to near nirvana for some readers and cooks.

> *2½ cups épeautre, or whole wheat berries*
> *3 tablespoons olive oil*
> *1 medium onion, minced*
> *2 quarts chicken stock*
> *Sea or coarse salt, to taste*

1. If using *épeautre,* soak it in warm water to cover for 10 minutes, then drain. If using wheat berries, soak them overnight in cold water to cover, then drain.

2. Heat the oil in a large skillet over medium-high heat. Add the onion and sauté until softened, 5 minutes. Stir in the *épeautre* or wheat berries and cook, stirring to coat the grains with the oil, for 3 minutes more.

3. Pour in all of the stock and bring to a simmer. Cover the skillet and cook over medium-low heat, stirring from time to time, until the grains are tender. If using *épeautre,* this will take from 50 minutes to 1 hour. Wheat berries take double or even slightly more time, and usually require draining the stock that fails to be absorbed during cooking. Fluff the hot grains, season with salt, and serve at once as you would rice.

Makes 8 servings

# A CYCLE IN CONTRASTS

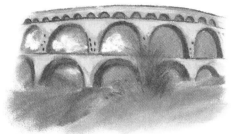

*T*he word *Provence* never fails to conjure up happy visions of a land flooded with sunlight and blessed with rich agricultural rewards, but when experiencing it by bicycle, one cannot help but notice that there are many distinctive and contrasting nuances to the five departments that make up the whole of Provence.

When I think of cycling in the areas west of St.-Rémy that we cover on our trips, I see a historic land of Roman relics such as the Pont du Gard aqueduct, Arc de Triomphe, and Ancient Theater in Orange, and the Palace of the Popes in Avignon. Heading closer to St.-Rémy, I feel the cool shade of Aleppo pines giving way to the arbored plane trees, tortured olive trees, and peaceful apricot orchards and melon fields that ring this friendly town. Climbing to Les Baux, I imagine the eleventh- and twelfth-century troubadours composing their poems of courtly love from the peaks of jagged Alpilles precipices and in the eerie, pebbled moonscape of the Crau plain. Arriving in the Lubéron, I become intoxicated by the prospect of relishing the best perched village scenery and mouthwateringly prepared food in all of inland Provence. It was in the Lubéron, after all, that I was first served and subsequently learned how to make chewy, nutty, and sensational *risotto d'épeautre*.

199

# rofé rice

**M**ention Provence's Carmargue and poster visions of expansive marshes and lagoons filled with bright pink flamin-
goes and galloping wild white horses come to mind. The eerie
wilderness of the Carmargue is also host to rice paddies where
the Rhône forms deltas as it empties into the Mediterranean.
While cuttlefish cooked with Carmargue rice is one of many rice
specialties from the area, I propose a much simpler side dish of
rice cooked with a healthy amount of crisp Provençal rosé wine,
about which I can never seem to rave enough. No wonder, for
the wine imparts a mysterious trufflelike taste to the cooked rice.
Domestic long-grain rice may be readily substituted for Carmargue rice.

> 2 tablespoons unsalted butter
> 1 medium onion, minced
> 1 cup minced fennel bulb
> 1½ cups long-grain rice
> 2 cups dry rosé wine, preferably from Provence
> 1 cup chicken broth
> ½ cup finely grated Parmesan cheese
> Sea or coarse salt and freshly ground black pepper,
>     to taste

1. Melt the butter over medium heat in a large, squat saucepan.
Add the onion and fennel and sauté until quite soft, 5 to 7 minutes.
Add the rice and stir to coat with the butter and vegetables.

2. Pour in the wine and the chicken broth; bring to a boil.
Lower the heat to a gentle simmer, cover the pan, and cook until

the rice is tender and all of the liquid has been absorbed, 20 to 25 minutes. Fold in the Parmesan, fluffing the rice with a fork, and season with salt and pepper. Serve at once.

mɑkeſ 6 ſervingſ

# roɑſted rɑtɑtouiLLe

Long before I ever pedaled voraciously alongside the fragrant melon vines, apricot orchards, lavender expanses, and silvery olive groves of Provence, I had simmered umpteen batches of the region's most famous vegetable dish, ratatouille. I had learned my technique for making ratatouille by following recipes in French cookbooks and my poetic inspiration from reading beautifully descriptive passages of the dish in M.F.K. Fisher's writings. The combination conspired to yield a recipe that closely resembled the ratatouilles I would later come to savor almost daily while traveling in Provence.

One day, however, seized by the craze for intensifying food flavors through high-temperature roasting, I took all of the usual ratatouille suspects—eggplant, zucchini, tomatoes, peppers, onion, and garlic—plus some additional favorites—asparagus, shiitake mushrooms, and new potatoes—and roasted them together. The results were at once so visually, aromatically, and gastronomically stunning that I now tend to cook only my stylized roasted version, and not the more traditional, simmered mash.

Roasted ratatouille makes a divine accompaniment to many

of the meat, poultry, and fish main dishes in this book. Leftovers, served at room temperature, make one of my favorite and frequent lunches or light suppers.

> 6 baby eggplants, about 4 inches long, stemmed and halved; or 1 large eggplant (about 1 pound), stemmed and cut into 1-inch-thick rounds
> 2 medium zucchini, stemmed, halved horizontally, each half cut lengthwise into 4 spear shapes
> 2 medium yellow squash, stemmed, halved horizontally, each half cut lengthwise into 4 spear shapes
> 1 red bell pepper, stemmed, seeded, and cut into 1-inch-wide strips
> 1 yellow bell pepper, stemmed, seeded, and cut into 1-inch-wide strips
> 8 small red-skinned potatoes, scrubbed and quartered
> 2 medium Bermuda onions, cut into ¾-inch-thick rings
> 8 large cloves garlic, peeled and halved
> 8 ounces shiitake mushrooms, stems removed and discarded
> Several sprigs of fresh rosemary
> ½ cup fruity olive oil
> Sea or coarse salt and freshly ground black pepper, to taste
> 8 ounces asparagus, tough ends trimmed and discarded
> 2 Belgian endive or small heads radicchio, quartered
> 2 medium ripe tomatoes, cut into 8 wedges
> ½ cup slivered fresh basil

1. Preheat the oven to 500°F.

2. Scatter the eggplant, zucchini, yellow squash, bell peppers, potatoes, onions, garlic, and mushrooms in a very large roasting pan (at least 16 × 14 inches) or two smaller pans (13 × 9 inches). Dot here and there with rosemary sprigs, drizzle and toss with the olive oil, and season with salt and pepper.

3. Roast the vegetables, stirring every 5 minutes, until very fragrant and almost tender, 25 to 30 minutes. Mix in the asparagus, endive, and tomatoes. Continue roasting, stirring once or twice more, until all the vegetables are tender, 10 to 12 minutes longer. Remove the pan from the oven and sprinkle with the basil. Serve the roasted ratatouille hot, warm, or at room temperature.

Makes 8 to 10 servings

## RATATOUILLE ROASTING ROSTER

When preparing a mix of vegetables, for high-temperature roasting, it is important to calculate roughly the varying cooking times of each individual vegetable, since the goal is to have them all become tender at the same time. Vegetables with a higher water content will cook more quickly, and thus logic dictates that peppers, zucchini, and eggplant be cut into larger or thicker shapes. Denser vegetables such as potatoes should be cut into smaller chunks. The most delicate vegetables—asparagus, endive, and tomatoes—must be added near the very end of the cooking time. Care also must be taken not to overcrowd the roasting pan, as crowding will cause the vegetables to steam rather than sear and brown. Finally, personal creativity should rule when undertaking a batch of roasted ratatouille as it is not necessary to include all the vegetables listed here. For example, the potatoes may be omitted for a lighter rendition, or the endive left out for those who may not care for its mild bitterness. Asparagus and tomatoes should be added only when in season.

203

## THE WORLD THROUGH A ROSÉ-FILLED WINEGLASS

*E*very sensitive traveler, whether or not familiar with Marcel Proust's celebrated *madeleine* passage, comes to associate specific food flavors and fragrances with places to which they yearn to return. For me, nothing epitomizes the beauty of Provence more than a cool glass or carafe of the region's pale, salmon-colored, breezy rosé wine, quaffed alfresco underneath a blazing midday sun. There's not a speck of seriousness to these pretty young wines, and that is precisely their Lolitalike charm. Unlike a scene-stealing, long-cellared Burgundy or Bordeaux, rosés from the South of France seem content to serve as blissful pockets of shade against the sun-drenched flavors of the area's fabulous cuisine.

Since American rosé, or even worse, blush wines have a deservedly bad reputation, there is always the initial challenge of convincing participants on my bicycle trips to drink like the locals. Experience has proven that a pedal up the formidable kilometers of the Tavel hill with the reward atop of an icy glass of the surrounding vineyard's highly regarded rosé is a surefire way to turn doubters into avid consumers.

Fortunately, the frivolous nature of these thirst-quenching wines precludes snobbery, but enthusiasts should definitely seek out the slightly more polished rosé bottlings from Château Romanin, outside of St.-Rémy, along with those from the famed vineyards of Bandol, Domaine Ot, and Domaine Tempier. Provençal rosés can be hard to come by stateside, though they are slowly becoming more popular as the craze for the health benefits of the Mediterranean diet makes inroads.

Whether your recreation emanates from the seat of a bike, or sunny summer deck, I've found the world to be that much more wonderful with a glass of happy-go-lucky Provençal rosé in hand.

# Sautéed Spinach with dried cranberries and toasted pine nuts

"**N**ecessity is the mother of invention" may be a clichéd adage, but it is one that conspired to make this recipe a real winner. One day when I was making the traditional recipe for Provençal sautéed spinach, in which the green is combined with currants, pine nuts, and orange flower water, I discovered in mid-sauté that I had no currants. Being the cranberry fiend that I am, I naturally had dried cranberries on hand and I substituted them—much to the delight of both eye and palate. While I'm fond of making and eating this intriguingly flavored spinach year-round, the contrasting red and green colors are of course particularly well suited to holiday entertaining.

205

½ cup dried cranberries
¾ cup warm water
1 tablespoon pastis, such as Pernod or Ricard
¼ cup olive oil
3 pounds fresh spinach, washed and trimmed of tough stems and veins
1 to 1½ teaspoons orange flower water (available
   in specialty food stores)
⅓ cup pine nuts, lightly toasted
Sea or coarse salt and freshly ground black pepper, to taste

1. At least 30 minutes before you plan to cook the spinach, place the cranberries in a small bowl and cover with the warm water

and *pastis*. Let soak for at least 30 minutes or longer. Drain before using.

2. Heat the olive oil in a large skillet over medium-high heat. Add the spinach and cook, tossing it constantly until wilted, 4 to 5 minutes. Sprinkle the greens with the orange flower water and then mix in the drained cranberries and pine nuts. Season all with salt and pepper. Serve at once.

makes 6 to 8 servings

# tomato eggplant fans

this splendid vegetable dish is both wonderful to behold and to consume. Thin wedges of sun-ripened tomatoes and bright green basil leaves are tucked in between fanned slices of plump little eggplants. The fans are then baked atop an olive oil-simmered and softened bed of onions and garlic strewn with bay leaves, thyme, rosemary sprigs, capers, and black olives. If I had to select one dish to capture the culinary essence of all the bountiful outdoor markets I've ever happened upon while cycling in Provence, this would be it.

½ cup fruity olive oil

2 large Spanish onions, thinly sliced

4 cloves garlic, minced

8 small eggplants (5 to 6 ounces each)

3 to 4 ripe beefsteak tomatoes

1 small bunch fresh basil

2 tablespoons drained capers

½ cup imported black olives, pitted and coarsely chopped

5 bay leaves

Several sprigs of fresh thyme

Several sprigs of fresh rosemary

Sea or coarse salt and freshly ground black pepper, to taste

1. Heat ¼ cup of the olive oil in a large skillet over medium-high heat. Add the onions and garlic and sauté until quite soft, 15 to 20 minutes.

2. Preheat the oven to 375°F.

3. Meanwhile, trim the stems from the eggplants and slice each 4 to 5 times lengthwise to within ½ inch of the stem end so that the uncut end holds the slices together to create a fan effect. Slice the tomatoes in half lengthwise and then into thin wedges. Slip 2 to 3 tomato slices in a row between the eggplant slices. Top each tomato slice with a whole basil leaf. Continue stuffing the eggplant in this fashion and repeat with remaining eggplants.

4. Mix the capers and black olives into the onion mixture and spread half of this mixture over the bottom of a large roasting pan (mine is 16 × 14 inches). Arrange the stuffed eggplant fans on top. Cover with the rest of the onion mixture. Tuck the bay leaves and the thyme and rosemary sprigs in and around all. Drizzle with the remaining ¼ cup olive oil and season generously with salt and pepper. Cover the pan tightly with aluminum foil.

5. Bake in the oven until the eggplants are tender, about 1½

hours. The fans may be served hot, warm, or at room temperature. Serve 1 eggplant per person and surround with plenty of the onion mixture.

makes 8 servings

# tomatoes provençale plus vites

208

**M**any believe these savory, bread-crumb-crisped baked tomatoes to be the truest symbol of the best homey Provençal cooking. These are the tomatoes to make in season on a daily basis, varying the choice of fresh herb to suit and complement other seasonings on the menu. Tarragon, thyme, basil, and mint all work well. Whether you choose to labor over the following recipe for Slowly Sautéed Summer Tomatoes à la Provençale or opt to feature this quicker recipe, you'll surely come to understand why tomatoes in old Provençal were called *puomos d'amour*—apples of love.

   *4½ tablespoons fruity olive oil*
   *8 medium firm ripe tomatoes, halved horizontally*
   *½ cup fresh French bread crumbs*
   *2 tablespoons fresh minced herb of choice (see above)*
   *3 tablespoons freshly grated Parmesan cheese*
   *Sea or coarse salt and freshly ground black pepper, to taste*

1. Preheat the oven to 375°F.

2. Heat 3 tablespoons of the oil in a large skillet over medium-high heat. When it is very hot add the tomatoes, placing them cut sides down and close together in the skillet. Sear them until the cut sides become caramelized to a deep brown, 5 to 6 minutes. Using a spatula, carefully transfer the tomatoes, cooked sides up, to a baking dish just large enough to hold them snugly side by side. Drizzle the cooking juices remaining in the skillet over the tops of the tomatoes.

3. Combine the bread crumbs, minced herb and Parmesan in a small mixing bowl. Moisten with the remaining 1½ tablespoons oil. Sprinkle this mixture lightly over the top of each tomato. Season with salt and pepper.

4. Bake the tomatoes until the tops are crusted brown, 25 to 30 minutes. The tomatoes may be served hot, warm, or at room temperature.

Makes 8 servings

# Slowly Sautéed Summer tomatoes à la provençale

In season, almost every dinner plate in Provence sports at least one cooked tomato half topped with some blend of bread crumbs, herbs, and garlic. But this old-fashioned recipe, where the tomatoes are sautéed at a snail's pace for 1½ hours, is the surest albeit slowest route to tomato heaven I know. Actually, it is not all that time-consuming when one considers the cooking takes four and a half hours less than a direct flight from New York to Nice!

Granted, there are quicker and less-attention-demanding ways of bringing a hot tomato to the dinner table (see the previous recipe), but every true tomatophile should try this old Provençal way of cooking vine-ripened tomatoes at least once.

8 medium ripe tomatoes
Sea or coarse salt
6 tablespoons fruity olive oil
2 teaspoons sugar
4 cloves garlic, minced
½ cup minced fresh parsley
¼ cup shredded fresh basil
Freshly ground black pepper, to taste

1. Cut the tomatoes in half horizontally. Using your index finger or a small spoon, scoop away as many seeds from the nooks and crannies of the tomatoes as you can. (The odd or stubborn remaining seed won't do anyone any harm.) Sprinkle the tomato cavities lightly all over with salt and then place them, cut side down, on a layer of paper towels to drain for 30 minutes.

2. Heat 4 tablespoons of the olive oil over medium-low heat in a heavy 12- to 14-inch skillet. Arrange the tomatoes, cut sides down, in a single, snug layer and sauté slowly, lowering the heat if the tomatoes start to brown too much, for 45 minutes. Carefully turn the tomatoes cut sides up and drizzle the tops with the remaining 2 tablespoons oil. Season by sprinkling evenly with a little more salt, the sugar, garlic, parsley, basil, and pepper. Cook over low heat for another 45 minutes. The tomatoes will be shriveled but still hold their shape. Serve the tomatoes, hot, warm, or at room temperature.

Makes 8 servings

# STARRY NIGHT
# SWEETS

MONT VENTOU

*N*OW I REALLY WANT TO PAINT A STARRY SKY. It often
seems to me that the night is still more richly coloured than the
day, having hues of the most intense violets, blues and greens.
If only you pay attention to it you will see that certain stars are
citron-yellow, others have a pink glow, or a green, blue and
forget-me-not brilliance. And without my expatiating on this
theme it will be clear that putting little white dots on a blue-
black surface is not enough.

—Vincent Van Gogh
writing to his sister, Wilhelmina

**M**ost desserts in Provence are very simple and centered on
delicious fresh fruit and nuts. Even the region's most
renowned dessert, known as the Thirteen Desserts and served
to conclude the Christmas Eve feast, consists of unadorned
almonds, hazelnuts, prunes, dates, raisins, figs, oranges, tanger-
ines, and special candied fruits made in and around the town of
Apt. Such simplicity is only fitting, since living, and that includes
biking, under Provence's potent sun, doesn't exactly inspire an
appetite for rich and ornate sweets. Serving a fruit tart or *clafoutis*
rather than a bowl of fresh fruit and platter of cheese is about
as fancy as it gets out in the countryside.

One wouldn't expect a land known for its dazzling daylight to have dull night skies, and it is when the Provençal night sky is at its brightest and most wildly Van Gogh-esque that the craving for a richer dessert or two surfaces. This is the time when the often talked about *mistral,* the violent and relentless northern wind that sweeps and howls down the Rhône valley, is likely to be blowing. It is said that the *mistral* was in full force in June of 1889 when Van Gogh painted *Starry Night.* And it is the shiver from memories of *mistrals* past and present that can make one hanker for a warm Plum Tarte Tatin or reassuring wedge of Chocolate-Orange-Pine Nut Tart mounded with a scoop of Lavender Honey Ice Cream.

213

# Seasonal Strawberry Tart

Open-air markets and roadside stands in Provence abound in May with red, red strawberries from areas surrounding the city of Carpentras. Local restaurants and bistros celebrate this seasonal bounty of *fraises de Carpentras* simply and frequently by offering classically French, short-crusted, custard-filled tarts topped with the ripest and juiciest local berries. The tarts are usually made just a few hours prior to serving and then consumed blissfully in their entirety.

The recipe is a good one to keep handy for the fleeting, pick-your-own strawberries time of year, and may also be made with raspberries as the summer progresses.

PASTRY CRUST
1¼ cups unbleached all-purpose flour
¼ cup (packed) light brown sugar
1 tablespoon grated orange zest
6½ tablespoons chilled unsalted butter, cut into
    small pieces
1 large egg yolk
1 tablespoon fresh lemon juice
½ teaspoon vanilla extract

CUSTARD
½ cup granulated sugar
¼ cup cornstarch
1 cup light cream or half-and-half
1 cup heavy (or whipping) cream
1½ teaspoons vanilla extract
2 large egg yolks, beaten in a small bowl

STRAWBERRY TOPPING
3 cups whole strawberries, hulled
½ cup red currant preserves
2 tablespoons orange-flavored liqueur

1. Preheat the oven to 375°F.

2. To make the crust, combine the flour, brown sugar, orange zest, and butter in a food processor and process until the mixture resembles coarse meal. In a small bowl, beat together the egg yolk, lemon juice, and vanilla. Add the mixture to the processor and process until the dough begins to form a ball. Turn the dough

into the center of a 10- to 11-inch tart pan with a removable bottom, and press it evenly over the bottom and up around the rim. Prick the bottom all over with the tines of a fork and then bake until lightly browned all over, 15 to 20 minutes. Let cool completely.

3. Make the custard: Combine all of the ingredients except the egg yolks in a medium-size saucepan. Cook over medium heat, stirring constantly, until smooth and thick, 4 to 5 minutes. Reduce the heat to low and continue cooking and stirring for 2 minutes more. Gradually stir ½ cup of the hot mixture into the beaten egg yolks, and then return this mixture to the saucepan, stirring constantly. Continue cooking over low heat until the custard is the thickness of mayonnaise, about 2 minutes. Pour the custard into a clean bowl, and let cool to room temperature, stirring occasionally. Cover and refrigerate until ready to use.

4. To assemble the tart, spread the custard evenly in the baked tart shell. Arrange the strawberries in concentric circles over the top. Heat the currant preserves and orange liqueur together in a small saucepan over medium heat until melted and smooth, 4 to 5 minutes. Gently brush the warm preserves over the berries to glaze them. Serve the tart at once or refrigerate until ready to serve. It should be eaten within 2 to 3 hours of assembling.

Makes 8 servings

215

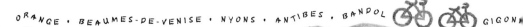
# plum tarte tatin

Apple *tarte tatin* is justifiably one of the most revered French desserts. The South of France, however, tempts with so many luscious, sun-kissed fruits that I can't resist the urge to replace the apples with juicier, more vibrant plums whenever Provençal fare is featured on my summer and early autumn menus. The plums impart a seductive, rich purple hue to the tart that recalls the intensity of the sealike expanses of blossoming lavender, whose billowing mounds illuminate the Provençal countryside in the heat of July. The festive flavor and presentation frequently persuade me to stick birthday candles in a plum *tatin* or two, rather than let my Cancer and Leo buddies eat cake after a *bourride* or *aïoli* feast.

216

The secret to making a successful *tarte tatin* is not to skimp on the fruit, since the dessert is essentially caramelized fruit inverted onto a thin, buttery, single-crust support. Warm slices of plum *tarte tatin* may be gilded with homemade Lavender Honey Ice Cream (see Index) or good store-bought vanilla ice cream.

PASTRY CRUST

1¼ cups unbleached all-purpose flour

8 tablespoons (1 stick) chilled unsalted butter, cut
    into small pieces

1 tablespoon sugar

½ teaspoon salt

1 tablespoon grated orange zest

2 to 3 tablespoons ice water

FRUIT FILLING

1 cup plus 3 tablespoons sugar

¼ cup water

6 tablespoons unsalted butter, cut into 6 pieces

20 to 24 firm, ripe purple plums

3 tablespoons orange-flavored liqueur

1. Make the pastry crust: Place the flour, butter, sugar, salt, and orange zest in a food processor and process until the mixture resembles coarse meal. Add the ice water and process just until the dough begins to ball together. Shape the pastry into a flat disk, wrap in plastic, and refrigerate for at least 2 hours.

2. To prepare the filling, combine 1 cup of the sugar with the water in a 10- or 11-inch cast iron skillet. Bring the mixture to a boil over medium heat and continue cooking until the sugar caramelizes to a light amber color. Remove from heat and stir in the butter pieces all at once, swirling to melt it.

3. Cut the plums in half and remove and discard the pits. Cut half of the fruit halves into quarters. Arrange the plum halves decoratively, skin sides down, on top of the sugar and butter mixture in the skillet. Fill in any gaps with quartered fruit. Keep in mind the *tarte* will be inverted after baking, so it is important to take care in arranging the bottom layer of fruit. Continue layering the rest of

the plums until they are almost level with the top edge of the skillet. Sprinkle the remaining sugar over the top.

4. Return the skillet to medium-low heat and cook until the syrup has thickened and the fruit has softened, 20 to 25 minutes. Be careful not to let the syrup or bottom layer of the fruit burn. If the plums seem to exude an excessive amount of juice that will dilute the syrup, then the excess (½ to ¾ cup) should be spooned off and discarded. Remove the skillet from the heat.

5. Preheat the oven to 400°F.

6. Roll out the pastry on a lightly floured surface to form a 12- to 13-inch circle. Place over the top of the skillet, trimming and crimping the edges to fit.

7. Bake the *tarte* until the pastry is golden brown, 30 to 35 minutes. Let cool 15 to 20 minutes, and then carefully invert onto a large, round serving platter. Serve warm. The *tarte* may be made early in the day and kept at room temperature. Reheat it in a 350°F oven until warmed through, 12 to 15 minutes.

ʍakeſ 8 ſervingſ

218

# Apricot and Almond cream tart

∞

In early March, the landscape where I live is often still a snow-covered one. At the same time of year in Provence, there is often a snowlike cover as well, but the white of this land comes from thousands of almond trees in blossom. Almonds were first brought to Provence hundreds of years ago by the Greek settlers and have appeared in the cuisine of the region ever since. While my groups unfortunately never cycle in Provence during almond blossom time, we do frequently pass by orchards dripping with apricots aplenty and have been known to leave a telltale marking of our day's route with a trail of pits. Billboards in Provence proclaim the apricot as "the orange of Provence," and when these "oranges" team up with the nuts produced, by March's snowy white blossoms, the merger is Provence-sent, if not heaven-sent.

PASTRY CRUST
½ cup slivered almonds, lightly toasted
3 tablespoons confectioners' sugar
1½ cups unbleached all-purpose flour
8 tablespoons (1 stick) chilled unsalted butter, cut into
    small pieces
Pinch of salt
1 large egg

FILLING AND FRUIT
½ cup slivered almonds, lightly toasted
½ cup granulated sugar
6 tablespoons unsalted butter, softened
1 large egg
1½ tablespoons kirsch liqueur
2 pounds firm, ripe apricots
½ cup confectioners' sugar, plus additional for dusting

1. Make the crust: Process the almonds and confectioners' sugar together in a food processor until the nuts are very finely ground. Add the flour, butter, and salt and process until the mixture resembles coarse meal. Beat the egg, add it to the processor, and process just

219

until incorporated and the dough begins to form a ball. Shape the crust into a flat disk, wrap it in plastic, and refrigerate for 30 minutes.

2. Preheat the oven to 400°F.

3. Roll out the pastry on a lightly floured surface to form a 12- to 13-inch circle. Ease it into a 10- or 11-inch tart pan, and trim and crimp the edges decoratively. Line the shell with aluminum foil and fill it with pie weights or dried beans. Bake the shell until just beginning to brown around the edges, about 15 minutes. Remove the foil and the weights and let the tart shell cool.

4. Make the almond cream filling: Process the almonds and granulated sugar together in a food processor until the nuts are finely ground. Add the butter, egg, and kirsch and process until the mixture is smooth and thick. Spread over the bottom of the cooled tart shell.

5. Pit the apricots and cut them into quarters. Arrange the apricots on top of the tart, cut sides up and close together. Sprinkle evenly with the confectioners' sugar. Bake the tart until the filling is set and the edges of the apricots are nicely browned, 30 to 40 minutes.

6. Serve the tart warm or at room temperature, dusted with additional confectioners' sugar.

Makes 8 servings

# chocolate-orange-pine nut tart

A long with almonds, pine nuts are the nut to appear most frequently in Provençal cooking. I've added chunks of bittersweet chocolate to the traditional Provençal pine nut tart because on chilly and starry nights when the *mistral* howls, a little indulgent melted chocolate strikes me as just the thing to follow the last warming sips of a red Rhône wine, such as a Châteauneuf-du-Pape or St.-Joseph. I particularly love to serve this tart with a scoop of Lavender Honey Ice Cream (see Index).

*PASTRY CRUST*
1½ cups unbleached all-purpose flour
⅓ cup granulated sugar
2 teaspoons grated orange zest
6 tablespoons chilled unsalted butter, cut into small pieces
2 large egg yolks
1 tablespoon chilled orange juice

*FILLING*
1 large egg, lightly beaten
⅔ cup heavy (or whipping) cream
2 tablespoons light brown sugar
6 ounces best-quality bittersweet chocolate, coarsely chopped
¾ cup pine nuts, lightly toasted

1. Make the crust: Combine the flour, sugar, orange zest, and butter in a food processor and process until the mixture resembles

221

coarse meal. Beat the egg yolks and orange juice together in a small bowl and add to the processor. Pulse the machine until the dough begins to gather into a ball. Shape the pastry into a flat disk, wrap in plastic, and refrigerate for at least 30 minutes. The pastry will keep for up to 2 days.

2. Preheat the oven to 375°F.

3. Roll out the pastry on a lightly floured surface to form a 12-inch circle. Ease it into a 10-inch tart pan with a removable bottom. Trim and crimp the edges of the tart decoratively. Prick the bottom of the tart all over with the tines of a fork. Line the tart with aluminum foil and fill with either pie weights or dried beans. Bake the tart for 15 minutes, lift off the foil and weights, and then return the shell to the oven and continue baking until lightly browned all over, about 10 minutes more. Let the shell cool for at least 10 minutes.

4. To make the filling, whisk together the egg, cream, and sugar. Pour into the tart shell. Scatter the chocolate chunks over the top and then sprinkle with the pine nuts.

5. Bake the tart until the custard is set and the top is golden, about 25 minutes. (The custard remains visible and browns between the chunks of chocolate, which do not melt enough to form a layer.) Let the tart cool to room temperature. Remove the rim from the tart before cutting into wedges.

Makes 8 servings

# ſtarry Night ſtarſ

ᘒ

the flavors in these cookies—orange, aniseed, and pine nut—mirror those of many other Provençal cookies, but the shape pays specific homage to Vincent Van Gogh's vision of a Provençal sky filled with "certain citron-yellow" stars. Dip these very Van Gogh stars into a glass of Muscat de Beaumes-de-Venise, perch them atop a scoop of Lavender Honey Ice Cream (see Index), or serve them alongside a bowl of freshly picked cherries, apricots, or figs.

8 tablespoons (1 stick) unsalted butter, softened
½ cup sugar
1½ teaspoons orange flower water (available in specialty food stores)
¼ cup fresh orange juice
2 cups unbleached all-purpose flour
Pinch of salt
2 teaspoons aniseeds
1 large egg beaten with
    1 tablespoon water
½ cup pine nuts

223

1. Using an electric mixer, cream the butter and sugar in a medium-size mixing bowl. Gradually beat in the orange flower water and orange juice. Using a wooden spoon, stir in the flour, salt, and aniseeds to make a smooth, semi-stiff dough. Shape into a flat disk and refrigerate for 30 minutes.

2. Preheat the oven to 375°F. Line 2 large baking sheets with parchment paper.

3. Roll out the dough on a lightly floured surface to a thickness of ⅓ inch. Cut into star shapes with a 1- to 1½-inch star-shaped cookie cutter. Arrange the cookies ½ inch apart on the prepared baking sheets. Brush lightly all over with the beaten egg mixture. Lightly press a pine nut into each of the 5 or 6 points on each star. Brush the cookies again with the egg mixture.

4. Bake the cookies until light golden brown, 12 to 15 minutes. Cool on a wire rack and store in an airtight container for up to 1 week.

Makes about 60 cookies

224

# Sabayon of Muscat de beaumes-de-venise

M uscat de Beaumes-de-Venise is the pale amber dessert wine of Provence. As the name indicates, it is made from the muscat grape in the quaint little Vaucluse town of Beaumes-de-Venise. There's not much for guidebooks to write about the town, but I always love to pause and taste the sweet wine on location in order to brace myself for the not-too-distant cycling climb to my night's accommodation at the luxurious hilltop Hostellerie de Crillon-le-Brave.

A small glass of chilled Muscat de Beaumes-de-Venise makes

a fine Provençal dessert in and of itself. The citrus-scented wine is also lovely poured into the hollow of a musky Cavaillon melon or cantaloupe. When a bit more festive dessert is in order, I like to make this silky muscat-based sabayon. If the weather is stifling, I'll chill the sabayon and lavish it over berries in parfait glasses and, perhaps, pass an accompanying plate of Starry Night Stars (see Index). If there's a nip to the night air, I'm inclined to pour the sabayon over a mix of seasonal fruits in a gratin dish and then broil all for a few minutes to caramelize the sugar and end up with a warm and creamy fruit compote.

225

4 large egg yolks

½ cup sugar

⅔ cup Muscat de Beaumes-de-Venise or other muscat
    dessert wine

½ cup heavy (or whipping) cream

1. Beat the egg yolks, sugar, and wine together in the top of a double boiler. Place over simmering water and whisk constantly until the mixture thickens and triples in volume, about 10 minutes. Remove from the heat and stir in the heavy cream.

2. If using in a fruit gratin, immediately pour the sabayon over the fruit and place in a preheated broiler for minutes. Otherwise, chill the sabayon in the refrigerator until cold.

Makes about 3 cups, enough for 6 parfaits or one 12-inch diameter gratin

# MIGNARDISES
## LES BORIES

**M**ignardises are delectable little sweets proffered after the meal and dessert at fancier French restaurants. The little tray of *mignardises* is often tiered and filled with breathtaking works of art in combinations of exquisite chocolate, spun sugar, and glistening fruit.

226

When our cycling groups stay at Les Bories in Gordes, we need little added inducement to linger late into the evening in the restaurant's lovely candlelit *borie*. Yet a rustic Provençal *mignardise* or two can certainly sweeten the approaching midnight hour. A favorite with my entire group during a recent stay could not have been simpler, more Provençal, or more delicious—moist prune halves stuffed with nuggets of rich almond paste and then rolled in white sugar. I recently ended a home-cooked Provençale fête in similar *mignardise* fashion, and the sweetmeats proved to be popular and conducive to midnight revelry. Prunes imported from Agen, in the southwest of France, make the most memorable *mignardises*.

# peAt ot Apple clAfoutiſ

A wonderful variation on the always comforting *clafoutis*—this one highlights either autumn's pears or apples embedded into a rich, flanlike custard.

2 cups milk
1 cup heavy (or whipping) cream
1 cup granulated sugar
1½ teaspoons vanilla extract
⅔ cup unbleached all-purpose flour
5 large eggs
6 Granny Smith apples or firm, ripe Anjou pears, peeled,
    cored, and thinly sliced
3 tablespoons brandy or fruit-flavored liqueur, such as
    Poires William, Calvados, or Grand Marnier
Confectioners' sugar, for dusting

227

1. Preheat the oven to 375°F. Generously butter a gratin dish 12 inches in diameter and 2 to 3 inches high.

2. Combine the milk, cream, sugar, and vanilla in a medium-size saucepan. Bring to a boil over medium-high heat, stirring to dissolve the sugar. Reduce the heat to medium and boil gently to cook slightly, 2 to 3 minutes. Remove from heat and set aside.

3. Place the flour in a medium-size mixing bowl, and using an electric mixer, beat in the eggs one at a time, scraping the sides of the bowl often, to make a smooth batter. Gradually beat in the warm milk mixture to form a smooth and thin batter. Pour into the prepared gratin dish.

4. Toss the apple or pear slices with the brandy and arrange in

layers over the top of the batter; they will sink down as you work. Bake the *clafoutis* until firm to the touch in the center and lightly golden on top, 1 to 1¼ hours.

5. Let the *clafoutis* cool to lukewarm or room temperature. Serve by cutting into pielike wedges, dusting each serving with confectioners' sugar.

Makes 8 servings

# pre-provence pineapple

during one spring recipe research trip to Provence, I made a point of traveling via New York so I could stop to attend a James Beard House brunch paying tribute to the influence of France on American cooking. The personable and creative executive chef from the Ritz Carlton in San Francisco, Gary Danko, prepared this most unusual, green-peppercorn-laced, fresh pineapple compote to kick off the brunch. I was so wowed by the sun-drenched sophistication of this unexpected combination that I felt transported to the Riviera a good forty-eight hours before my flight actually departed JFK for Nice.

This is my take on Gary's recipe, and I find it equally provocative when served as an eye-opener for lazy weekend entertaining or a light ending to a lush evening of Provençal feasting.

1½ cups dry white wine
¾ cup sugar
3 tablespoons drained brine-packed green peppercorns
2 ripe pineapples, peeled, cored, and sliced into ¾-inch-thick rings
½ cup fresh mint, slivered

1. In a heavy saucepan, bring the wine and sugar to a boil over medium-high heat. Boil, stirring to dissolve the sugar, until the liquid is perfectly clear and syrupy, 2 to 3 minutes. Stir in the green peppercorns and remove from the heat. Let cool to room temperature.

2. Combine the pineapple and syrup in a large bowl, stirring gently to coat the fruit. Refrigerate for several hours or overnight to let the flavors marry and mellow. Just before serving, stir in the mint. Spoon the pineapple with some of its marinade into fruit bowls or wide glass goblets.

Makes 10 to 12 servings

229

# Lavender Honey ice cream

there wasn't a dish I didn't want to make at home after my simply wonderful May meal at Le Comptoir du Victuailler in Gordes. So I can't think of a better way to end this book than with my favorite essence of Provence, as captured in the rich and creamy ice cream scooped forth at one of my favorite restaurants in the prettiest of Provençal perched villages.

2 cups half-and-half
½ cup lavender or other wildflower honey
2 tablespoons untreated fresh or
    dried lavender blossoms
6 large egg yolks
½ cup sugar
1½ cups heavy (or whipping)
    cream

1. Combine the half-and-half and honey in a medium-size saucepan and bring to a boil over medium heat, stirring to incorporate the honey. Add the lavender blossoms and cook 1 minute more. Remove from the heat and let the blossoms steep in the mixture for 1 hour. Strain the blossoms from the mixture and discard. Return the strained mixture to the stove and heat until hot to the touch, but not boiling.

2. Using an electric mixer, beat the egg yolks and sugar together in a medium-size bowl until thick and pale. With the mixer on low, slowly add 1 cup of the hot mixture to the yolks to temper them. Combine the yolk mixture with the rest of the hot cream in the saucepan. Stir this mixture gently and constantly over medium heat until it forms a custard thick enough to coat the back of a spoon, 7 to 10 minutes. Take care not to let the mixture boil.

3. Stir the heavy cream into the custard and then refrigerate until cold. Transfer the chilled custard to an ice cream maker and process according to the manufacturer's instructions. The honey in the ice cream may cause the mixture to take a little longer than normal to freeze and will make the ice cream slightly softer. Store the ice cream in the freezer and scoop whenever the craving strikes.

Makes about 1 quart

# Index

∽

231

233

235

# Q, R

# S

239